SHORTER WALKS IN
THE DOLOMITES

ABOUT THE AUTHOR

Gillian Price was born in England and moved to Australia when young. She took a degree in anthropology and then worked in adult education before moving to Venice, which she had visited as a student and to which she had vowed to return permanently.

Gillian now lives there with her husband, Nicola, a native Venetian, and works as a writer and translator, including stints for the Venice Film Festival.

Venice is only two hours from the Dolomites. Starting there, Gillian has steadily explored the mountain ranges of Italy and brought them to life for visitors in a series of outstanding guides for Cicerone. Her next project is a guidebook to Corsica.

Other Cicerone books by the author:
Walking in the Central Italian Alps
Walking in the Dolomites
Walking in Italy's Gran Paradiso
Walking in Sicily
Walking in Tuscany
Treks in the Dolomites Alta Vie 1&2 (with Martin Collins)

SHORTER WALKS IN THE DOLOMITES

by
Gillian Price

2 POLICE SQUARE, MILNTHORPE, CUMBRIA, LA7 7PY
www.cicerone.co.uk

© G. Price 2002
ISBN 1 85284 351 9
A catalogue record for this book is available from the British Library.

'A traveller who has visited all the other mountain-regions of Europe, and remains ignorant of the scenery of the Dolomite Alps, has yet to make acquaintance with Nature in one of her loveliest and most fascinating aspects' J. Ball, *Guide to the Eastern Alps* (1868)

To my wonderful parents, Bet and Dave, on their 50th wedding anniversary.

Acknowledgements
The Fondazione Antonio Berti in Venice generously made available a copy of J. Gilbert and G.C. Churchill's fundamental 1864 work *The Dolomite Mountains: Excursions through Tyrol, Carinthia, Carniola, and Friuli*.

As usual, Nicola Regine excelled himself in mapmaking.

Advice to Readers

Readers are advised that while every effort is taken by the author to ensure the accuracy of this guidebook, changes can occur which may affect the contents. It is advisable to check locally on transport, accommodation, shops, etc, but even rights of way can be altered.

The publisher would welcome notes of any such changes.

Cover photo: Saltnerhütte and the Sciliar's Punta Santner (Walk 26)

CONTENTS

Introduction

Background 11
When to Go 14
Getting There 15
Local Transport 16
Maps 17
How to Use this Guide 18
What to Take 21
Weather and Forecasts 23
Emergencies 23
Information 24
Accommodation 24
Food and Drink 26
Protected Areas 27
Wildlife 28
Vegetation 30

Walks

1 – Fanes-Sennes-Braies Park: Lago di Braies 37
2 – Fanes-Sennes-Braies Park: Rif. Biella and Croda del Becco 41
3 – Fanes-Sennes-Braies Park: M. Specie 45
4 – Dolomiti d'Ampezzo Park: Alpe di Sennes Circuit 48
5 – The Old Calalzo–Dobbiaco Railway Line 53
6 – Sesto Dolomites: Croda Rossa di Sesto Traverse 57
7 – Sesto Dolomites: the Val Fiscalina Tour 60
8 – Sesto Dolomites: Tre Cime di Lavaredo Circuit 65
9 – Sesto Dolomites: Monte Piana 69
10 – Cadini di Misurina Loop 74
11 – Sorapiss: Rif. Vandelli Traverse 77
12 – Antelao–Marmarole: Val d'Oten 81
13 – Spalti di Toro-Monfalconi: Rif. Padova to Rif. Tita Barba 85
14 – The Pramper Circuit 89
15 – The Pelmo and the Dinosaur Footprints 92
16 – Around the Croda da Lago 97

17 – Up the Nuvolau 101
18 – Lagazuoi Piccolo: First World War Tunnels 105
19 – Settsass Circuit 110
20 – Santa Croce Sanctuary 114
21 – Puez–Odle: Sass de Putia Circuit 119
22 – Puez–Odle: Sentiero delle Odle 124
23 – Puez–Odle: Roving Across the Altopiano 128
24 – Puez–Odle: Rasciesa and Geological Phenomena 133
25 – Alpe di Siusi: The Bulacia 137
26 – Alpe di Siusi: Rif. Bolzano 140
27 – Castello Presule 144
28 – Circumnavigating the Sassolungo-Sassopiatto 147
29 – Sella: Piz Boè circuit 152
30 – The Sass d'Adam Crest 157
31 – Marmolada: Rif. Falier 160
32 – Viel del Pan 163
33 – Civetta, the Northwestern Flank 168
34 – Pale di San Martino: A Circuit on the Altipiano 174
35 – Pale di San Martino: Rif. Mulaz 180
36 – Latemar: Lago di Carezza and the Labyrinth 184
37 – Catinaccio: the Inner Realms of the Rose Garden 188
38 – Catinaccio: Sentiero del Masaré 194
39 – Brenta Group: Rif. Tuckett and ai Brentei Tour 197
40 – Brenta Group: the Glories of Val d'Ambiez 202

Italian–German–English Glossary 207

Further Reading 209

Legend

═══	motorway
───	sealed road
▬ ▬ ▬	walk route
▭▭▭	walk route via sealed road
───	unsealed road
▬▬ ▬▬	walk route via unsealed road
⋯⋯⋯	walk variant
┼┼┼┼┼	railway

②	walk number
🞂	crest
🏠	hut/hotel accommodation
🏰	castle
✝	church, shrine or cross
•──▭──•	cable-car
•──●──•	gondola car
•──▣──•	chair lift

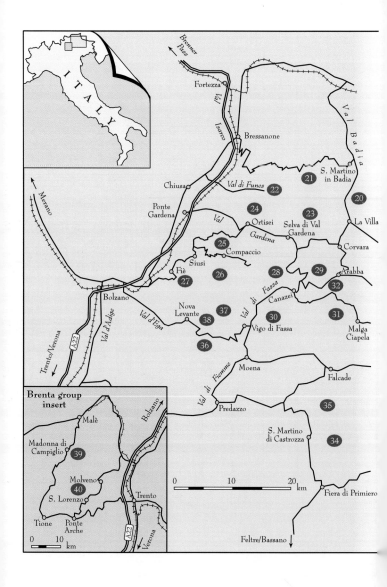

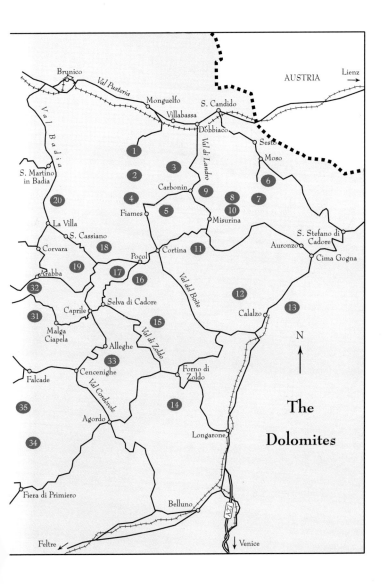

Brunico
Val Pusteria
Monguelfo
Villabassa
S. Candido
AUSTRIA
Lienz →
Val Badia
Dobbiaco
Sesto
Moso
S. Martino
in Badia
①
②
③
Carbonin
④
Fiames
⑤
⑨
⑧
⑦
⑥
⑩
Misurina
⑳
La Villa
S. Cassiano
⑱
Pocol
Cortina
⑪
S. Stefano di
Cadore
Auronzo
Corvara
Arabba
⑲
⑰
⑯
Selva di Cadore
⑫
Calalzo
Cima Gogna
⑬
㉜
㉛
Caprile
⑮
Malga
Ciapela
N
↑
Alleghe
Val di Zoldo
Val del Boite
Falcade
㉝
Cencenighe
Forno di
Zoldo
㉟
Val Cordevole
⑭
The
Agordo
Longarone
Dolomites
㉞
Fiera di Primiero
Belluno
A27
Feltre ←
↓ Venice

Val Sassovecchio with Cima Una (Walk 7)

INTRODUCTION

BACKGROUND

BACKGROUND

'Here the traveller obtains a view of the Dolomite Mountains. They are unlike any other mountains, and are to be seen nowhere else among the Alps. They arrest the attention by the singularity and picturesqueness of their forms, by their sharp peaks or horns, sometimes rising up in pinnacles and obelisks, at others extending in serrated ridges, teethed like the jaw of an alligator; now fencing in the valley with an escarped precipice many thousand feet high, and often cleft with numerous fissures, all running vertically.'

Murray's Handbook, quoted in J. Gilbert and G.C. Churchill, 1864

Like the Alps to which they belong, the Dolomite mountains were long regarded with awe and a good dose of fear by the populations of herders and woodcutters who clustered around their bases. It was not until the 1800s and the advent of 'travelling', that the first leisure-seeking visitors, Britons for the most part, ventured through treacherous passes to glimpse the wonderful scenery and enjoy the breathtaking *enrosadira* sunsets. Published accounts and guidebooks began to appear, and soon both tourists and mountaineers from all over Europe flocked there to conquer the magnificent heights, untrodden until then except by the odd chamois hunter.

North face of the Tre Cime from Rif. Locatelli (Walk 8)

Rif. Re Alberto beneath the Torri del Vaiolet (Walk 37)

Nowadays the Dolomites mean a prime holiday destination in both summer and winter, with superbly located resorts connected by good roads and equipped for all pockets. An ultra-modern system of space-age cable-cars and lifts whisks visitors to dizzy heights in a matter of minutes, extending the range of short routes (not to mention easing steep descents). On the other hand, nature lovers will be delighted by the vast expanses of magnificent forests, high-altitude rockscapes and seas of wild flowers. Only a little effort is needed to get away from the 'hot spots' and spend days in solitude on the marvellous network of paths that link hospitable mountain huts.

The sheer, pale rock in bizarre fantastic formations, unique spectacular aspect of the 'Pale Mounts', as they were first known, attracted geologists well before the travellers. In 1789 French mineralogist Déodat Guy Sylvan Tancred Grated de Dolomieu identified the composition of the principal rock as the limestone variant calcium magnesium carbonate, later named dolomite in his honour. As regards its origin, scholars puzzled over the abundance of fossilised shells and marine creatures embedded in the rock at such heights and so far from the sea. The theory of the Flood long rejected, in 1860 German scholar Baron Ferdinand von Richthofen proposed their genesis as a coral reef, work further developed by Edmund von Mojsisovics. While the sedimentary nature of dolomite is undeniable, there continues to be disagreement over the nature of its mutation from regular limestone. The earliest theory on how the newly discovered rock was actually formed came from Leopold von Buch in the 1820s. He suggested that the magnesium-rich vapours released from molten volcanic rocks penetrated the limestone, transforming it into the white dolomite rock, a theory not completely discounted to this day. In the meantime, researchers in Brazil, for instance, have suggested the efforts of industrious bacteria in tropical environs.

In general terms, the rocks were formed some 230 million years ago when a shallow tropical sea covered the area. Deposits of corals and sea creatures gradually built up on the sea floor. It was not until 65 million years ago that the area underwent the dramatic tectonic events that led to the creation of the alpine chain as rock slabs were up-ended and lifted hither and thither. Glacial sheets and erosion from snow, rain and wind continue to shape the wonderful mountains visitors see today.

One additional noteworthy natural phenomenon widely observable in the Dolomites is karstification, named after a limestone area in Slovenia. Carbon dioxide in rainwater reacts with limestone and causes it to dissolve over time, leading to the formation of characteristic sink holes, fissures, curious grooved rock surfaces (karren) and a notable absence of surface water, which reappears at the foot of the mountain, often as a waterfall.

In addition to natural beauty, the valleys of the Dolomites offer attractions ranging from old-style farms still run according to ancient traditions to towns such as Trento, Bolzano and Bressanone that boast priceless art treasures and make for a fascinating visit on that rainy day. Settlements date back to prehistoric times, as attested by the excavations at Mondeval (Croda da Lago), and the area's history is punctuated with a series of heavy-handed dominators and determined ongoing rebellion. Early peoples fleeing barbaric invaders made their homes in the relative protection of the high-altitude mountains, and succeeded in conserving their original language: the ancient Rhaeto-Romanic language known as Ladin has survived to this day and is the declared mother tongue of 4.3% of the inhabitants of the northernmost South Tyrol (Alto Adige). However, this region, which accounts for a third of the Dolomites, is dominated by the German language (68.2% of the population), the legacy of sixth-century invaders and cultivated under the Austrian Hapsburgs. Along with the adjoining Italian-speaking Trentino, it has been part of Italy since 1919 in the wake of the First World War, and now enjoys a privileged political and economic status as one of Italy's autonomous regions. The remaining southeastern chunk of the Dolomites is administered by the Veneto region, based in Venice. Centuries before, during the glorious era of the Serenissima Republic, immense rafts of timber were piloted downstream to the city for use in its foundations and shipbuilding.

'The Dolomites! It was full fifteen years since I had first seen sketches of them by a great artist not long since passed away, and their strange outlines and still stranger colouring had haunted me ever since. I thought of them as every summer came round; I regretted them every autumn; I cherished dim hopes about them every spring.'

Amelia Edwards, 1873

Visit the Dolomites between June and October for walking, unless you're equipped with snowshoes or skis for the marvellous snow season: Christmas to Easter. From early summer many low-altitude walks are feasible and the paths quiet, though it's worth waiting

Old wartime Felizon rail bridge (Walk 5)

At the Croce di Dobbiaco on M. Piana (Walk 9)

until well into July for high-altitude routes to be free of late-lying snow, as this accumulates in gullies and can conceal waymarking or turn into icy stretches. Several other factors condition walking: the *rifugi* huts open from late June through to late September (should you rely on them for overnight accommodation or meals), while bus services run from about late June to September (see local transport below). August can bring scorching conditions and is also the busiest month, with the peak Italian vacation period focusing on August 15th, a national holiday. It is advisable to book accommodation in advance at this time. July is the best month for flowers, while September to October means cooler conditions and superb visibility as autumn and its crispness approaches. Late-season walkers will be rewarded by improved

chances of observing wildlife in solitude. Italy stays on summer time until the end of October, when there is daylight until about 6pm.

GETTING THERE

The Dolomite mountains are in the northeastern part of Italy bordering Austria. They occupy a parallelogram that extends across the regions of Trentino–Alto Adige (South Tyrol) and the Veneto. The main block is bordered by the Val Pusteria in the north, S. Stefano di Cadore and the Piave river valley in the east, a line connecting Belluno, Feltre and Trento in the south, then the busy Adige–Isarco river valley running up through Bolzano and Bressanone, with the appendage of the Brenta group near Madonna di Campiglio in the west.

By plane: The nearest international airports are at Verona and Venice, Innsbruck in Austria and Munich in southern Germany.

By car: Via Europe's extensive motorway system, the best entry to Italy is by the Brenner Pass from Austria on the A22 autostrada. This leads directly to the northwestern Dolomite district in the South Tyrol, with handy exits from Bressanone southwards. Otherwise leave the A4 Turin–Trieste via a link near Verona for the A22 north. From Mestre (outside Venice) the quiet A27 runs up via Vittorio Veneto, with good roads continuing for Belluno and towards Cortina for the eastern Dolomites.

Good national roads, labelled SS for *Strada statale,* cover the inner regions, and relevant details are given in the access paragraph for each walk in this guidebook.

By train: International lines serve the stations south of the Brenner Pass, as well as Verona to Venice. Useful branch lines via Belluno or Vittorio Veneto reach Calalzo, while for the Val Pusteria change at Fortezza, north of Bressanone.

By bus: Long-distance coaches from major north Italian cities such as Genoa (STAT-Turismo), Milan (Autostradale), Bologna (Best Bus) and Venice (ATVO, Brusutti and Dolomiti Bus) provide convenient links with the Dolomites throughout both the summer and winter seasons. See the following section for contact phone numbers.

LOCAL TRANSPORT

A good many of the walks in this guide start and end at a point that is accessible by local public transport, mostly buses. The bus network is surprisingly extensive, inexpensive and unfailingly reliable, while the drivers know the mountain roads and conditions like the back of their hand. Visitors are invited to leave their car at home or hotel and use these services, thus not contributing to air pollution and traffic congestion in these magical mountains. Many holiday resorts offer free or cut-price bus passes for their guests to encourage this habit. Following are the main companies (bus and train) and the areas they cater for:

- Atesino (Trentino) tel. 0461-983627
- ATVO (Venice–Cortina) tel. 041-5229773
- Autostradale (Milan–Val Badia) tel. 0471-836176
- Best Bus (Bologna–Venice–Val Badia) tel. 800-237237
- Brusutti (Venice–Caprile, San Martino and others) tel. 041-929333
- Dolomiti Bus (Belluno province) tel. 0437-941167 or 0437-941237
- FS (Ferrovia dello Stato) State rail services tel. 8488-88088
- FTM – Ferrovia Trento–Malè tel. 0461-431111 (Val di Sole link to Madonna di Campiglio)
- Holzer tel. 0474-710309 (San Candido–Val Fiscalina)

- SAD and all South Tyrol/Alto Adige public transport, tel. 800-846047 or web site www.sad.it
- Saita (S. Stefano di Cadore–Passo Montecroce Comelico–S. Candido) tel. 040-425001
- STAT-Turismo (Genoa–Val Badia) tel. 0142-781660

Note: for Atesina and SAD services, tickets are sold on board. The €5 pass (one-year time limit) available from SAD is economical for multiple passengers and trips. Dolomiti Bus tickets should be purchased beforehand (bars, tobacconists, etc) and stamped on the bus, otherwise a surcharge is applied.

Operating periods for buses as well as cable-cars, etc, are listed in the Access section of each walk itinerary, but need to be taken with a pinch of salt as they can vary widely from year

to year depending on weather conditions, school vacation periods and how public holidays fall.

In the absence of a bus, enquire at the tourist office or a local café for a taxi. Charges are usually in the vicinity of €0.50 per kilometre.

MAPS

An excellent network of paths penetrates the Dolomites, each marked with frequently placed red/white paint stripes on prominent fence posts, tree trunks and rocks, and complete with its own distinguishing number. These are marked on the commercial maps, though there is the odd annoying discrepancy. While sketch maps are provided in this guide, it is imperative that walkers obtain the recommended commercial maps listed in the walk

Casera Vedorcia and the Monfalconi (Walk 13)

Bridge across Torrente Talagona (Walk 13)

heading and widely available both in the Dolomites and from leading outdoor specialists and bookstores overseas. The sketch maps supplied in the guide are simplified representations only, and cannot show watercourses and other features necessary for orientation in case of emergency or if planning an escape route. Moreover the commercial maps enable distant landmarks such as settlements and important peaks to be identified, a fascinating and rewarding exercise.

The brand Tabacco and 1:25,000 scale (priced at about € 5) are by far the best on the market at present, with clear art work. Their only drawback is the recent trend in reintroducing ancient place names, usually in the Ladin version, which correspond neither to local usage nor signposting. The older 1:50,000 scale maps are also available and cover more territory with a single purchase, though understandably with less detail. Otherwise there are the Kompass or Mapgraphic brands, though the former in particular uses crude colouring and often imprecise colour overlays.

Place names in the Dolomites often come in trilingual versions. For the purposes of this guide the Italian version has been given preference, followed by the German where deemed useful. There is an Italian–German–English glossary of topographic and other features at the back of this guide.

Plenty of good road maps can be found – the Touring Club Italiano 1:200,000 Trentino Alto Adige is hard to beat.

HOW TO USE THIS GUIDE

Exploring the Dolomites embraces a vast array of terrains, ranging from gently undulating farmland through to forest carpeted with soft needles, as well as plenty of rugged rockscapes with near vertical routes on mountainsides and mobile scree slopes. Everyone should plan on some preparatory fitness training. While there's little an Australian bushwalker or British hillwalker can do in the way of sheer 1000m ascents, any sports activity will aid general stamina and make a walking holiday in the Dolomites more enjoyable.

The red and white waymarkings along the route are referred to in the walk description as n.1, etc. Each walk has an accompanying sketch map (the

Aided stretch climbing to Passo del Ball (Walk 34)

circled numbers on the map refer to the corresponding walk).

The routes chosen for this guide are purposefully 'short' and all are feasible in a single day, with the advantage that little luggage is needed. However, most become even more enjoyable if stretched out over two days, with an overnight stay in one of the huts identified in the walk description. The walks in this guide distinguish a 'track', which is vehicle-width, a 'path', which is narrower and strictly people only, and a 'road', surfaced or otherwise, which takes four-wheeled traffic. Longer multiple-day routes can be found in *Walking in the Dolomites* by Gillian Price (Cicerone Press, 1991). The information at the start of each walk includes details of walking time, difficulty and ascent/descent.

Difficulty for the walks has been classified in grades, however adverse weather conditions will make any route more arduous. Even a level road can be treacherous if icy.

- Grade 1 – an easy route on clear tracks and paths, suitable for beginners.
- Grade 2 – paths across typical mountain terrain, often rocky, where a reasonable level of fitness is preferable.
- Grade 3 – strenuous and requiring experience, often entailing exposed stretches and extra climbs.

Note: A number of walks described here have stretches across rock faces aided by anchored cable. While experience is clearly preferable, they are not

Lago d'Antorno and the Cadini (Walk 10)

strictly climbing routes and do not necessitate special equipment. However a number of rules need to be followed.

- Always keep away from iron cables and rungs in bad weather and if a storm is brewing, as the fixtures attract lightning.
- Avoid two-way traffic on a single stretch of cable as it can become awkward and consequently dangerous trying to pass people.
- It's common sense to wait until people approaching from the opposite direction have passed before you proceed, which also avoids added strain on cables.

Timing given in the walk headings is strictly walking time only and does not include stops for rests, lunch, photographs, etc. An extra hour or so must always be added when planning a day's programme.

If following a route in the opposite direction, allow roughly ⅔ of the time if it's an ascent that you're descending, and about 1½ times more for a downhill section that you're climbing up.

Ascent/descent is also given (in metres) in the walk headings. This is important information, as height loss and gain are indicative of the effort required and an ascent–descent factor should be summed to difficulty when planning the day. An averagely fit walker will usually cover 300m (about 1000ft) in ascent in one hour.

Altitude in metres above sea level (abbreviated as m) is used in the descriptions for all the key locations and reference points encountered, and should not be confused with minutes (abbreviated as min).

Toilet stops: the best rule is to wait until the next hut and use their facilities. Where this is unavoidable, try and keep well away from watercourses to minimise pollution, and under no circumstances leave unsightly (and unhygienic) toilet paper or tissues lying around. Bury everything in consideration for other visitors and animals, but without causing unnecessary damage. Resist the temptation to use caves, rock overhangs and abandoned huts to relieve yourself as someone may need to take shelter there in bad weather!

WHAT TO TAKE

Essentials start with good quality waterproof boots incorporating ankle support and non-slip soles, and preferably not brand new, unless you protect your feet with sticking plaster. Trainers are definitely not sufficient. Next is a comfortable rucksack, roomy enough to contain food and drink for a day, along with rain gear and emergency items including a first-aid kit. A must are a sun hat, glasses and very high factor protective cream – remember that for every 1000m of ascent, the intensity of the sun's UV rays increases by 10%. Clothing is needed to cater for fiery sun through to lashing rain and storm conditions, which may include snow.

Baita Segantini and Cimon della Pala (Walk 35)

Lightweight telescopic ski poles are a handy optional item for descending steep slopes and easing the weight load of a rucksack off knees and back.

Always carry a full day's supply of water as chances are not high of finding any en route. At some huts the water is undrinkable (*non potabile*) as supplies come from snow-melt or glaciers, often unsuitable in terms of salt content. Unless you use the water from streams in pasture zones, bacterial contamination is not usually a problem, so purification tablets may not help. Safe bottled mineral water (*acqua minerale*) as well as a range of hot and cold drinks can always be purchased at the huts.

Mineral salts are helpful in combating salt depletion caused by profuse sweating; unexplained prolonged fatigue and symptoms similar to heat stroke indicate a problem.

Although food and drink is usually available at huts on the majority of walks described here, never rely on them, but always be self-sufficient and carry generous amounts of your own; bad weather, minor accidents and all manner of unforeseen factors could hold you up on the track, and that extra biscuit or sip of water could become crucial.

For an overnight stay in a hut visitors will need slippers to change into, as boots must be left on racks in the hall. A sleeping sheet is compulsory in the huts run by the Alpine Clubs (see Accommodation section, below). A fair range of gear can be found at village markets and specialist shops throughout the Dolomites.

Note: whatever your style of walking and personal needs, don't overload your rucksack unnecessarily as a painful back can detract significantly from pleasure from a mountain experience. Weighing your pack before setting out is a useful exercise.

WEATHER AND FORECASTS

During summer in the Dolomites visitors can expect full days of blazing hot sun, hopefully tempered by cool breezes, wild electrical storms with dramatic lightning displays and lashing rain, which are more often than not followed by brilliant clear skies and cool crisp conditions. The odd snow fall is not to be discounted in high spots. A bit of everything, in other words!

Daily weather bulletins are posted at many tourist offices, hotels and mountain huts. Take forecasts seriously and don't embark on a walk in unsettled conditions. As a general rule, start out early in the morning to give yourself plenty of daylight.

An altimeter can help for predicting conditions – when the reading for a known altitude inexplicably goes up, this means that the atmospheric pressure has dropped and weather could turn bad; the opposite also holds true.

The following web sites could be useful: www.meteoalpin.com has succinct reports in German, Italian and English covering the Veneto and South Tyrol regions, and www.arpa.veneto.it/csvdi/bollettino will get you a detailed forecast of the Veneto Dolomites and foothills, but only in Italian at present.

EMERGENCIES

The mountain rescue services (*soccorso alpino*) can be activated by phoning 118 throughout the Dolomites (whereas the general emergency number is 113). Members of the Italian Alpine Club (CAI) and affiliated associations have insurance cover for rescue operations, while others may find themselves shelling out for hefty bills, especially if a helicopter is involved. Insurance for alpine activities is worth investigating before departure from your home country.

Should help be needed during a walk, use the following internationally recognised rescue signals: SIX signals per minute either visual (waving a handkerchief or flashing a torch) or audible (shouting or whistling), repeated after a pause of one minute. The answer is THRFF visual or audible signals per minute, to be repeated after a one-minute pause. Anyone who sees or hears a call for help must contact the nearest mountain hut, police station, etc, as quickly as possible.

These hand-signals could be useful for communicating at a distance or with a helicopter.

Both arms raised diagonally

- help needed
- land here
- YES (to pilot's question)

One arm raised diagonally, one arm down diagonally

- help not needed
- do not land here
- NO (to pilot's question)

the Dolomites, www.dolomiti.it/eng is fairly helpful and provides a range of information mostly relative to the Italian-speaking areas, with accommodation and links for regional weather forecasts.

INFORMATION

The Italian Tourist Board in London can help intending travellers with general information: 1 Princes St, London W1R 8AY, tel. 0171 408 1254.

Local tourist offices for all the Dolomite valleys and locations referred to in the walks are listed at the end of each route description, and have full details of cable-cars, local transport and accommodation, camp sites, etc. Of the burgeoning web sites covering

ACCOMMODATION

There's a vast choice of hotel (*albergo*) and bed & breakfast (*affittacamera*) options in all the Dolomite valleys. The South Tyrol villages tend to be more economical – look for *zimmer frei/ camera libera* (room free) signs. Reservation in key resorts such as Cortina is not usually necessary outside the August peak season. The phone number for relevant tourist offices is listed at the end of each walk descrip-

Lunch at Rif. Malga Brogles backed by the Odle (Walk 22)

tion, along with selected guesthouses in the vicinity of the start or finish point.

Details of *Rifugi* (abbreviated Rif.), or manned mountain huts, are also given in the route description. Set in spectacular high-altitude positions accessible only to walkers or climbers (with the odd exception at road level), these marvellous establishments are open all through the summer and offer reasonably priced meals and sleeping facilities varying from spartan dormitories with bunk beds to simple guest-house standard rooms. An overnight hut stay can be a special part of a walking holiday. Charges are around €17, without food. Many are run by CAI, the Italian Alpine Club, as well as its Trento section (SAT) if not the South Tyrol club (AVS), and are open to everyone. Members of affiliated alpine associations from other countries get good discounted rates (50% for a bed; 10% off meals) in line with reciprocal agreements. Pillows and blankets are always provided, so sleeping bags are not needed. Sleeping sheets, however, are compulsory in the club-run huts, so carry your own unless you don't mind purchasing one in cotton or lightweight synthetic akin to paper (both re-usable and machine washable) or paying a supplement to cover laundry. You'll also need a small towel, not that hot or cold showers are common. A pair of lightweight running shoes or slippers is good idea as boots cannot be worn inside the huts, though guests are sometimes provided with rubber flip-flops. Hut rules include 'lights out' from 10pm to 6am and no smoking unless in specially designated areas. If you plan an early morning start, it's a good idea to pay your bill the evening before to save time.

Rifugio accommodation should be booked in advance July–August, especially on weekends for the hot spots. When you phone, tell the guardian: 'Vorrei prenotare un posto letto/due posti letto' (I'd like to book one/two beds). Be aware that a booking can set costly (for you) emergency search procedures in motion if you don't turn up, so remember to cancel if you change your plans. Furthermore, get into the habit of signing the hut register and including your next day's schedule, or leave word at your hotel of your planned route.

The occasional ultra-modern *rifugio* establishment accepts credit cards, but it's best to carry a sufficient amount of euros in cash, to be on the safe side.

Camping should be restricted to official valley sites, though a discreet pitch well off a path and away from the huts should not be a problem. The advantages of camping include solitude, in welcome contrast to some of the crowded huts, not to mention flexibility, while the main drawback is the extra weight of the equipment you need to carry. Remember that wild camping is not allowed in the protected park areas.

Using the Phone: Telecom's orange-silver public phones can be found dotted throughout many a village, otherwise ask at the nearest café or bar for *un telefono pubblico*. Get yourself a prepaid phone card from a paper shop or bar and remove the dotted corner before use. When dialling, remember to include the area code complete with its '0', even for a local call – the only exceptions are toll-free or cell phone numbers. All the *rifugi* have a phone, usually available for guests.

FOOD AND DRINK

While this may not be the gastronomical heart of Italy, gourmets will not be disappointed. Some memorable wines hail from the Dolomite valleys: amongst the reds are the full-bodied Teroldego and lighter Schiava from the Trentino, and Blauburgunder (Pinot nero) from the slopes around Bolzano.

The whites are headed by the heavenly aromatic Gewürztraminer which reputedly originated at Termin, close to Bolzano, while very drinkable white Rieslings and similar are grown on the steep terraces over the Isarco valley.

Refreshing on a hot summer's day is *Holundersaft*, elderberry blossom syrup. Coffee on the other hand is strictly Italian style and comes as short black espresso, milky frothy cappuccino and an infinite intermediate range.

In terms of food, the northern valleys pride themselves on delicious cereal breads, such as the crunchy rounds of unleavened rye bread with cumin seeds, *Völser Schüttelbrot*, or a softer yeasty version. Both are a perfect taste match for thinly sliced *Speck*, a

Capanna Fassa on Piz Boè (Walk 29)

The Cinque Torri formation (Walk 17)

local type of smoked ham flavoured with juniper berries, coriander and garlic. Ask at the bakeries for *Apfelstrudel* or *Mohnstrudel,* a luscious pastry roll stuffed with apple or poppy seeds respectively.

Knödelsuppe (*canederli in brodo*) consists of traditional farm-style dumplings the size of tennis balls, made of bread blended with eggs, flavoured with *Speck* and served in consommé. With any luck, the pasta course will be *Schlutzkrapfen,* light home-made ravioli filled with spinach.

For main course *Tosella* is definitely worth tasting – a fresh cheese vaguely resembling mozzarella, it is lightly fried in butter then quickly oven-baked with cream. Otherwise go for *Polenta con formaggio fuso,* corn meal smothered with melted cheese, and possibly accompanied by *funghi,*

wild mushrooms. Meat eaters can order spicy goulash or variations of *Bauernschmaus,* smoked pork and sausages on a bed of warm *crauti* (*Sauerkraut*).

For those with a sweet tooth, the dessert front is dominated by *Kaiserschmarm,* a rich concoction of sliced pancake with dried fruit and redcurrant jelly. Another special treat and a meal in itself is *Strauben,* fried squirts of sweetened batter with bilberry sauce.

PROTECTED AREAS

Set up in 1993, the long overdue Parco Nazionale Dolomiti Bellunesi spreads across the wild ranges in the far south of the Dolomites (Headquarters at Feltre, tel. 0439-3328). Around the same time in the Cortina district the

Male ibex on Croda del Becco

Dolomiti d'Ampezzo park (info point, Fiames, tel. 0436-3031) appeared as local administrations became more environmentally enlightened. Both are making up for lost time with excellent education programmes, forest and fauna management and upkeep of paths. Earlier on, protected areas (*parchi naturali*) were established under regional jurisdiction by the financially better-off Alto Adige–Trentino. These are the Sesto Dolomites, Fanes-Sennes-Braies (combined visitors' centre at Dobbiaco, tel. 0474-555457, May–Oct), Puez-Odle, Sciliar, then Paneveggio-Pale di San Martino (summer visitors' centres at Paneveggio, tel. 0462-576283; Val Canali, tel. 0439-64854; San Martino, tel. 0439-768859) and Adamello-Brenta (summer visitors' centres at Daone, tel. 0465-674989, and Spormaggiore, tel. 0461-653622).

One fairly useful web site, www.parks.it, gives a general picture of many of Italy's regional and national parks.

The general aim of the parks is to protect and preserve unique alpine zones and habitats, with special zoning applied for traditional farm activities. As in mountain environments the world over, in the parks visitors are asked to adhere to simple common-sense rules such as no camping, no fires, no dogs (even on a leash) and no picking flowers. Any rubbish should be carried back to villages and resorts for disposal; this gives staff time for more important tasks.

WILDLIFE

One of the beauties of walking is the chance to observe the surprisingly abundant wildlife that inhabits these mountains. The easiest sightings are o marmots: adorable furry social creatures a bit like beavers that live in extensive underground colonies and hibernate from October to April. They often forage for their favourite flowers on grassy slopes, only returning to the safety of their burrows on the shrill warning cry of their omnipresent sentry, an older figure standing stiff and erect on some prominent rock.

The widespread conifer woods provide shelter for roe deer, though often only a fleeting glimpse of them is seen due to their shyness. Higher up, seemingly impossible rock faces and scree slopes are the ideal terrain for herds of fleet-footed chamois, mountain goats with short hooked horns. A more impressive if rarer creature is the majestic ibex, sporting trademark sturdy grooved horns. Due to over zealous hunters they became extinct in the Tyrol as early as the 17th century, however healthy nuclei survived in both a royal game reserve in Italy's Valle d'Aosta and the Engadine in Switzerland. Specimens were brought back to Dolomite habitats some 30 years ago, and there are well-established groups around the Croda del Becco and at the 'rear' of the Marmolada.

A more recent example of reintroduction, hopefully as successful, regards seven brown bears from Slovenia, sent in recent years to supplement the dangerously low nucleus in the Adamello-Brenta park.

Man has introduced livestock such as cows, goats and sheep, encountered on high-altitude pastures in summer, along with the striking sturdy chestnut Haflinger horses. Of the 6000 worldwide, over half are in the South Tyrol, such as Val Gardena and the Alpe di Siusi.

Birdwatchers will enjoy the delightful small song birds in the conifer woods, while a number of sizeable birds of prey such as kites, buzzards and golden eagles are occasionally spotted above the tree line. One special treat is the showy high-altitude wallcreeper. Fluttering over extraordinarily sheer rock faces in its hunt for insects, it flashes its black plumage with red panels and white dots, and attracts attention with its shrill piping whistle. Then there is the ptarmigan, a type of high-mountain grouse that nests on grassy slopes and makes sounds a bit like a pig snorting. In winter, with a perfect white plumage camouflage, it can patter over snow surfaces without sinking thanks to fine hairs on its claws, akin to snowshoes. However the queen of the feathered species is undoubtedly the rare capercaillie, a proud if cumbersome dark ground bird similar to black grouse which inhabits conifer woods.

Warning: There are two potential dangers. The first comes in the shape of bites from ticks (*zecche*), the occasional one of which may carry Lyme's disease and even TBE (tick-borne encephalitis), life-threatening for humans in rare cases. The problem is limited to the Feltre-Belluno districts and applies to heavily wooded areas with thick undergrowth. Sensible precautions include wearing long light-coloured trousers which show up the tiny black pinpoint insects more easily, and not sitting in long grass. Inspect your body and clothes carefully after a walk for any suspect black spots or undue itching, a sign of a tick which may have attached itself to you. However before attempting tick removal by grasping the head with tweezers, take the time (5 minutes) to cut off its air supply by applying a cream such as toothpaste or oil and oblige it to loosen its grip. If in any doubt, don't hesitate to go to the nearest hospital, where an antibiotic may be prescribed as a precaution.

The second warning concerns vipers (adders), smallish light grey snakes with a diamond-patterned back.

Their bite can be fatal, particularly for children and the elderly, however this is an extremely rare occurrence. Though widespread, especially in abandoned pasture around huts, where they thrive in the absence of rats, they are timid creatures and slither away very quickly if in danger. They only attack if threatened, so if confronted with one on a path, for example, give it ample time and room to escape. A pocket-sized battery-operated device Ecobite (available from Ecobrands, UK) is currently the most effective system for dealing with bites from a viper. It delivers a series of mini electric shocks which evidently cause the venom to decompose, as well as alleviating discomfort.

Haymaking huts, southeast side Sass de Putia (Walk 21)

The elegant martagon lily

Alpenrose shrubs brighten mountain slopes

Lady's slipper orchid, maroon petals around a yellow lip

VEGETATION

The Dolomite area boasts some 1500 species of glorious flowering plants, a quarter of the total found in Italy as a whole. They alone are a good reason to go walking in summer. Heading the list is the mythical edelweiss, found in alpine meadows, felty petals forming delicate overlapping stars. Though not especially eye-catching, its blanched aspect inspired the legend that it was brought down from the moon by a princess, a memory of the pale lunar landscape to which she was accustomed.

Unmissable, fat and intensely deep blue trumpet gentians burst through the grass, and there are also daintier star-shaped varieties. Pasture zones also feature orange lilies and the wine-red martagon variety which vie with each other for brilliance. Stony grass terrain is often colonised by alpenrose bushes, rather like the azalea, with masses of pretty red-pink flowers in late July.

Of the earliest blooms to appear is the alpine snowbell, its fragile fringed lilac bells visible in snow patches, never far away from hairy Pasque flowers in white or yellow. Shaded clearings are the place to look for the unusual lady's slipper orchid, recognisable for a sizeable yellow lip receptacle crowned by maroon petals, while masses of purple orchids are common in meadows. Gay Rhaetian poppies punctuate dazzling white scree slopes with their patches of bright yellow, never far from clumps of pink thrift or round-leaved pennycress

Bulbous gentians

Pink cinquefoil blooms appear amidst silver-grey leaves

Round-leaved pennycress thrives on apparently barren scree

The unmistakable brilliance of king-of-the-Alps

which is honey scented. A less commonly encountered flower is the king-of-the-Alps, a striking cushion of pretty bright blue blooms, reminiscent of a dwarf version of forget-me-not. A rare treat is the devil's claw from the Rampion family, whose pinkish lilac flower with curly pointed stigma specialises in vertical rock faces. Another rock coloniser is saxifrage, the name literally 'rock breaker'.

A couple of flowering plant species are endemic to the Dolomites. Moretti's bellflower (*Campanula morettiana*), with its rounded deep blue petals, nestles in rock crevices between 1500 and 2300m, while the succulent Dolomitic houseleek (*Sempervivum dolomiticum*) prefers sunny dry slopes and sports a bright green stalk and deep pink pointy flowers.

In terms of trees, beech grow up to about the 1000m line before the conifers take over. Silver fir, spruce and several types of pine tree mingle with the Arolla pine, which can reach 2600m in altitude and is recognisable for its tufted needles and reddish bark. A further notable is the springy low-lying dwarf mountain pine, a great coloniser of scree, while another high achiever (up to 2500m) is the larch, the sole conifer to lose its needles in autumn in a copper-tinged rain.

The unusual bear's-ear

Lago Crespeina on the Puez plateau (Walk 23)

1 – Fanes-Sennes-Braies Park: Lago di Braies

Walking time	1hr 30min
Walk distance	3.5km/2.2 miles
Difficulty	Grade 1
Map	Tabacco n.031 scale 1:25,000
Start point	Hotel Lago di Braies

Romantic Lago di Braies (or Pragser Wildsee) is held by many to be the most beautiful lake in the Dolomites, and is a hard one to beat. It boasts deep emerald-green waters bounded by bleached shingle beaches and sheer cliffs that plunge into the cool depths. Lying at the foot of towering 2810m Croda del Becco (or Seekofel) mountain, which is reflected on the still surface, it owes its existence to ancient rock falls which barred the valley. The name may be linked to the Celtic term 'bracu', which refers to a marsh or swamp. On the other hand it is believed to have originated from the Ladin word for trousers, as the south-running valley forks evenly into 'trouser legs'.

Various types of trout survive in the lake's chilly depths, which plunge to a maximum of 36m, while the surface temperature rarely exceeds 14°C. Located at 1496m above sea level and covering some 31 hectares, the lake is fed by numerous alpine streams and several underground springs. As a rule it ices over in late November and reverts to liquid form only around May. It is always peaceful as motor-propelled craft are forbidden – the area comes under the Fanes-Sennes-Braies Nature Park. In winter the lake can be reached on cross-country skis.

A marvellous establishment adorns the northernmost end in the shape of the grand grey stone Hotel Lago di Braies/Pragser Wildsee. It first saw the light of day 130

According to an old Ladin legend, every 100 years on a full moon night the blind Queen of Fanes and her daughter Princess Dolasilla leave their underground dwelling beneath the Sass dla Porta (also known as Croda del Becco) via a secret doorway. Their subjects slumber on in the depths of the mountain, while the two row across the Braies lake in the hope of hearing silver trumpets announce the dawning of the promised time and the rebirth of their kingdom. Alas, they row in vain.

Lago di Braies in its steep-sided basin

years ago as a modest refreshment point; this gradually developed into a restaurant and then into a grand hotel around 1897–9. A little later, in the 1960–70s, it hosted meditation sessions courtesy of the Beatles' personal guru, Maharishi Mahesh Yogi. Despite all manner of questionable renovations over the years, it is still a marvellous place to stay. Most rooms have retained their old-style furnishings, with massive ornamental wash basins and admirable antique toilet chains. Meals are served in the magnificent spacious Art Nouveau dining rooms by armies of uniformed waiters.

This walk route consists of an anti-clockwise stroll around the lake, a delight for all age groups. Alternating waterside strolling with paths through the wood and endless picnic opportunities, it is straightforward with negligible ascent/descent, and a leisurely hour and a half is sufficient for the 3.5km.

As a suitable follow-up either embark on an exploratory scull over the water in one of the lovely rowing boats for hire, or treat yourself to tea or an aperitif in the hotel garden.

A longer, more demanding route starting at the lake is described in Walk 2.

AROUND THE LAGO DI BRAIES (1HR 30MIN RETURN)

From the bus stop, go right and follow the rear of the rambling **Hotel Lago di Braies** (1496m) to the start of the Giro del Lago, namely signed pathways n.1/4. A wide level route at first, it strikes out south past a chapel along the western border of the lake, shaded by towering pines and brightened by alpenrose. As you approach the far extremity, the forestry track itself veers right (west) up Val di Foresta into the Colli Alti group, while you depart from it and move around onto the beach, with a backing of dwarf mountain pines. A little further on, where n.1 turns up south for the 800m climb to Rif. Biella, you keep to the open lakeside (n.4 now), below notable rivers of scree flowing from eroding gullies on the face of Croda del Becco. Directly opposite the hotel, at the halfway point on the walk, is a marvellous spot for a dip on a sultry summer's day, though, in view of the water temperature, only for the courageous.

Rounding the lake's corner for the start of the northward leg, you soon find yourself in light deciduous wood beneath the rocky mass of the Piccolo Apostolo. A modest waterfall is soon encountered, then a series of steps and raised timber walkways lead around a pretty

Access to start point:
Lago di Braies is served by daily SAD bus in summer (3rd week June to mid-September) from Dobbiaco/Toblach via Villabassa/Niederdorf in Val Pusteria/Pustertal. At other times of year the service is limited to S. Vito/St. Veit, 3km down the road. Drivers will find the appropriate turn-off midway between Monguelfo/Welsburg and Villabassa, however be warned that high fees are charged at all the car parks in the vicinity of the lake.

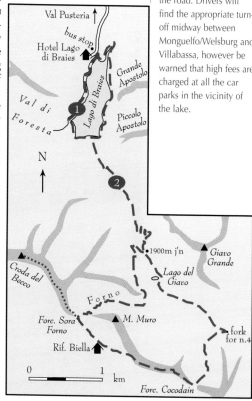

Tourist Office Braies/Prags tel. 0474-748660

Tourist Office Villabassa/Niederdorf tel. 0474-745136

Hotel Lago di Braies/Pragser Wildsee tel. 0474-748602 open May–Oct, special rates for walkers

rocky point below the Grande Apostolo, affording a lovely view over the lake.

Soon the path loops around a shallow marshy backwater, reminiscent of a slender outreached finger often edged by thick yellow buttercups. Then you pass the landing stage with the hired rowing boats before returning to the premises of **Hotel Lago di Braies.**

Lakeside path, Lago di Braies

2 – Fanes-Sennes-Braies Park: Rif. Biella and Croda del Becco

Walking time	5hr 30min + 2hr for Croda del Becco
Walk distance	16.5km/10.2 miles
Difficulty	Grade 2 (Grade 3 for Croda del Becco)
Ascent/descent	950m/950m (450m extra for Croda del Becco)
Map	Tabacco n.031 scale 1:25,000
Start point	Hotel Lago di Braies

The 'elephant' itself (see right) is climbed in the course of this walk, which starts out from the 'small lake', namely Lago di Braies (or Pragser Wildsee). A memorable picture postcard alpine lake with turquoise-emerald waters, it is fringed with peaceful beaches and sheer cliffs. An especially photogenic landmark stands at the northernmost extremity – the marvellous old-style Grand Hotel in grey stone which has retained a hint of its former glory.

The area as a whole belongs to the Fanes-Sennes-Braies Nature Park, something of a haven for wildlife. Though bears, wolves and lynx were effectively wiped out in the late 1800s, there are still plenty of animals to see: playful marmots, chamois grazing on open rocky hillsides, roe deer in the cover of the woods and a range of trout in the lake. Encounters with the stately ibex are guaranteed for those who venture up the Croda del Becco (also known as Seekofel and Sass dla Porta). Centuries after they were hunted to extinction, the majestic creatures were successfully reintroduced in the 1970s from the thriving colonies which breed freely in the Gran Paradiso National Park, on the Italian side of M. Blanc.

The walk itself is a lengthy and tiring circuit, requiring abundant drinking water and sun protection.

'If an excursion is made to Ausser Brags, a noble view is presented of the massive square-edged wall of the See Kofel, impending over a small lake, and rising to a height of 9,200 feet. Its upper beds belong to the Jura formation, and are stained with red, as are portions of many of the neighbouring peaks. Its dark form, as seen from Cortina, when backed by storm clouds, looks marvellously like a gigantic elephant uprearing itself.'
(J. Gilbert and G.C. Churchill, 1864)

The first stage follows the opening stretch of popular long-distance path Alta Via 1 as far as Rif. Biella, a great spot for lunch; however, on the return loop there's little chance of meeting anyone else. The optional Croda del Becco ascent – highly recommended and extremely rewarding – entails a further 450m climb on a partially exposed and aided route, unsuitable for inexperienced walkers.

A shorter easy loop around the lake is described in Walk 1, along with more details on the lake itself, legendary and otherwise, while Walk 4 approaches Rif. Biella from the south.

Access to start point: | **STAGE ONE: FROM LAGO DI BRAIES TO RIF. BIELLA (3HR)**

see Walk 1.

Behind **Hotel Lago di Braies** (1494m) is a sign for n.1 and Rif. Biella. The broad track through shady pines follows the lake edge south to a shingle beach at the base of massive Croda del Becco. Soon path n.1 breaks off south-east (30min) to cross extensive scree flows where dwarf mountain pines and alpenrose have taken root. You climb steadily nearing the eastern flanks of Croda del Becco, zigzags taking the sting out the slope, and the odd bench providing relief. A crumbling cliff face is rounded thanks to a reinforced wooden walkway and chain, then after a rise is the **1900m junction** with n.4 (where the return route links up) and the arrival of a steep short cut direct from the lakeside. Keep straight on at n.1.

The wood is much thicker and shadier now, and the lake is left well behind as you penetrate the inner silent valleys. After a fork left is ignored (2186m, path n.3), the path enters the forbidding corridor aptly named Forno, a 'furnace' on scorching summer days when the towering rock flanks block out any hope of a breeze. The going is relentless to say the least.

You eventually emerge at the minor pass **Forcella Sora Forno** (above the furnace, 2388m), a short distance above the refuge on the edge of a plateau. This is the start point for the optional but highly recommended ascent to the Croda del Becco, if you feel up to a further 450m climb. It entails a partially exposed aided stretch which may feel more difficult in descent.

Optional ascent of Croda del Becco (2hr return time)
A must on a good day for anyone with a head for heights
and an appreciation of spectacular views. You zigzag up
the steep southeastern corner of the mountain and soon
reach fixed chain where the path is a little exposed along
near vertical rock strata. The top section is wider and
levels out somewhat, keeping to the left side of the crest,
with cairns marking the way. It becomes surprisingly
grassy and you may see the rock grouse that nest here, if
not the well-established herd of ibex that graze peace-
fully ignoring the tourists. A cross marks the summit of
Croda del Becco (2810m, 1hr 15min), a simply breathtaking spot where 360° views take in a surprising number
of Dolomites including Picco di Vallandro to th east and
the Tre Cime di Lavaredo further back, the Tofane to the
south and even the Puez altopiano to the southwest, not
to mention the lake at your feet and the snow-capped
Austrian ranges spreading across the northern horizon.

*Rif. Biella at the foot of
Croda del Becco*

Return the same way, taking extra care on the aided section.

From **Forcella Sora Forno** in 10min you reach the cream stone building **Rif. Biella** (2327m), an exemplary old-style refuge, whose generous slices of home-made mouth-watering tortes and *Apfelstrudel* are hard to resist.

STAGE TWO: TO FORCELLA COCODAIN (30MIN) AND DESCENT TO LAGO DI BRAIES (2HR)

Path n.28 entails a gradual ascent east to a rocky crest studded with edelweiss. As you're a little way back from Croda del Becco now, its regular onion-skin layers of limestone are clearer, as is its crazily tilted 45° angle. The airy ridge followed here means wonderful outlooks, including a bird's-eye view of Lago di Fosses, below the Remeda Rossa. Watch your step, though, as the way is pitted with hollows where precious soil has collected and an astonishing range of blooms such as pink cinquefoil flourish.

From **Forcella Cocodain** (30min, 2332m) a faint route leads due north down the regular rock strata thick with wildflowers, and marked by occasional red and white paint stripes. After some 20min or so of clambering you join path n.3 (2210m) and turn right. Only minutes away is a signed **fork for n.4** and Lago di Braies, and it leads easily down northwest into a grazing basin populated by cows. This valley is lined by curious inclined rock slabs run through by the grooves and channelling typical of karstification. Past a diminutive lake, Lago del Giavo, the valley narrows, and you drop to rejoin n.1 at the **1900m junction** (1hr from Forcella Cocodain).

(Here, as an alternative to the path followed in ascent, plunge straight down for the more direct knee-jolting route to the lakeside.)

Once back down on the water's edge, inviting for a dip, keep right for the delightful path along the rocky eastern shore. A waterfall is passed, then a raised walkway leads around a rocky point, before the marshy northern-pointing finger and return to **Hotel Lago di Braies** (1494m, 2hr 30min from Rif. Biella).

Tourist Office Braies/Prags tel. 0474-748660

Tourist Office Villabassa/Niederdorf tel. 0474-745136

Hotel Lago di Braies/Pragser Wildsee tel. 0474-748602 open May–Oct, special rates for walkers

Rif. Biella tel. 0436-866991 CAI, sleeps 45, open 25/6–30/9

3 – Fanes-Sennes-Braies Park: M. Specie

Walking time	2hr 45min
Walk distance	10km/6 miles
Difficulty	Grade 1–2
Ascent/descent	320m/320m
Maps	Tabacco n.03 or 010 scale 1:25,000
Start point	Rif. Pratopiazza

Pratopiazza is one of those rare perfect alpine basins dotted with pines and inhabited by photogenic dairy cows and timber chalets, but with the extra appeal of being bounded by a number of spectacular Dolomites. Set at 2000m above sea level and soaked in sunshine, Pratopiazza lies in the Fanes-Sennes-Braies Nature Park and doubles as a beautiful cross-country ski arena in winter; it also acts as the start point of this walk. However the actual goal is 2307m Strudelköpf (also known as Monte Specie or Heimkehrerkreuz), a self-effacing promontory overlooking the middle section of Valle di Landro between Cortina and Dobbiaco, an easy 'summit' for everyone, though strangely not that well known. The views are astonishing, prevalently onto the Sesto Dolomites; in clear weather conditions, try and be there in the late afternoon to catch the best colours.

Both meals and refreshments are served at the two *rifugi* en route as well as an old-style classy hotel at Pratopiazza, though any picnic fare will need to be purchased beforehand, back down in Val Pusteria.

A recommended follow-up is the considerably more strenuous path directly behind Rif. Pratopiazza leading up 2839m Picco di Vallandro, a more famous panoramic point. The final stretch entails some exposure and requires a sure foot, otherwise the 2hr30min climb is trouble-free, if a little monotonous.

The pointed Picco di Vallandro rises above Pratopiazza to the north, while opposite is the majestic deep-red Croda Rossa, 'our blood-stained "Mount of sacrifice"' for Gilbert and Churchill (1864). However, an ancient and politically questionable tale attributes the colour to the rock blushing in sympathy with an orphan brought up by marmots in the caves on the mountain: after the inevitable marriage to a handsome prince, the girl was deliberately embarrassed by a jealous noblewoman who revealed her humble background.

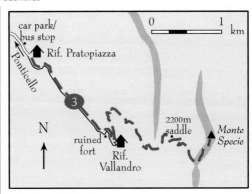

Between Monguelfo/
Welsberg and Villabassa/
Niederdorf in Val
Pusteria/Pustertal take
the signed road that turns
off south for Braies/Prags.
A few km along ignore
the fork right for Lago di
Braies and keep straight
on for Ponticello/
Brückele. From here the
next 7km are narrow and
steep in parts and closed
to private vehicles in
midsummer – a special
shuttle bus (10/7–20/9)
runs to Pratopiazza/
Plätzwiese. SAD buses
also cover the
Dobbiaco/Toblach–
Ponticello stretch late
June–late Sept.

STAGE ONE: TO RIF. VALLANDRO (30MIN)

From **Rif. Pratopiazza** (1991m) a wide 4WD track marked
as n.37 cuts southeast across the pastoral basin dotted
with red-barked Arolla pines. Remember to close the livestock gates behind you. Backed by the Cristallo group,
ruins of a prominent Austrian fort stand out ahead,
reminders of the activity in the area during the 1915–18
conflict. Close by stands friendly **Rif. Vallandro** (2040m).

STAGE TWO: ASCENT OF M. SPECIE (1HR)

On the uphill side of **Rif. Vallandro** you need n.34, an
old military road with a rough white stone surface. (Fit,
impatient walkers can embark on the steep short cuts,
signed 'Heimkehrerkreuz'). You wind easily in ascent
amongst dwarf mountain pines, eventually narrowing to
a path heading southeast. After heading over a ridge,
there's a brief drop towards the ruins of a barracks at a
2200m saddle (40min), where you are joined by a variant
from Val di Landro. The final 20min to the top – recognisable due east with its cross – sees you cutting
obliquely a regular slope. It is not until the very last
moment that the rounded top of **M. Specie** (2307m)
reveals its breathtaking magic: straight across the valley
to the east is the wild Rondoi-Baranci group, then the Tre
Cime, slender and sharp like knife-blades from here, and
enhanced by the special evening shadows. Slightly
further afield are the Cadini to the southeast and the

Marmarole beyond, as well as the Cristallo due south and the Tofane to the southwest.

STAGE THREE: DESCENT VIA RIF. VALLANDRO (45MIN) AND RIF. PRATOPIAZZA (30MIN)
Return the same way you came.

The Croda Rossa from Pratopiazza

Tourist Office Braies/ Prags tel. 0474-748660

Hotel Croda Rossa tel. 0474-748606

Rif. Pratopiazza/ Plätzwiesehütte tel. 0474-748650 private, sleeps 50

Rif. Vallandro/ Dürrensteinhütte tel. 0474-972505 private, sleeps 22

4 – Dolomiti d'Ampezzo Park: Alpe di Sennes Circuit

The ancient hunting castle of S. Uberto used to stand on a prominent hillock just off the main road from Cortina and, as the story goes, belonged to two dignified English ladies who were forced to abandon it with the outbreak of the First World War. Set in no-man's land, in the early days of the conflict its well-stocked cellar received regular visits from both Austrian and Italian troops under the cover of night, though nothing as slight as a skirmish ever broke out according to the older hands, each side preferring to stagger back in silence to its respective camp loaded with precious provisions. At a later date the castle was shelled to smithereens, only the place name surviving on maps at the narrow mouth of the beautiful valley leading to the Alpe di Sennes uplands, the destination of this walk.

Walking time	5hr 20min (reducible to 3hr) + 1hr 30min on foot from S. Uberto
Walk distance	17km/10.5 miles
Difficulty	Grade 1–2
Ascent/descent	830m/830m + 250m/250m from S. Uberto
Map	Tabacco n.03 scale 1:25,000
Start point	Rif. Ra Stua

This walk to the Alpe di Sennes uplands entails a good range of scenery and habitats, and two neighbouring nature parks – Dolomiti d'Ampezzo and Fanes-Sennes-Braies – are traversed, home to veritable hordes of ibex, chamois, roe deer and marmots, as well their inevitable 'companion' birds of prey. Grandiose Dolomite groups headed by the Croda Rossa are foremost features, their lower flanks cloaked by flourishing woods of a healthy mix of evergreen conifer and deciduous species. A visit is feasible throughout the year, starting with ski tourers and snowshoers in the more rigid months, then right through the glorious summer to October, a magical time for the stunning russet hues and golden 'rain' from the larch trees. Four particularly hospitable *rifugi* are included and make marvellous lunch or refreshment stops.

Stages One and Two mostly follow clear easy tracks, while Stage Three uses a rather steep path for the final descent. Families with small children should find several sections suitable, if they ever get past the central valley where the attractive gurgling streams seem to act as a magnet on youngsters.

A marvellous follow-up is a visit to the Cascata di Fanes with its 70m drop, held to be the highest in the

Dolomites. Access is via the car park and visitors' centre a short distance north of Fiames.

STAGE ONE: VIA CAMPO CROCE (20MIN) TO RIF. FODARA VEDLA (1HR)

Rif. Ra Stua (1668m) is a worthwhile destination in itself, a cosy hut-cum-dairy farm set amidst an ample picturesque valley running between the Croda Rossa (east-northeast) and Lavinores (west) Dolomite groups. The name Stua comes from 'dam' – the nearby stream used to be blocked to operate machinery for the medieval quarry of red stone next to the hut. Further up the slope, don't miss the magnificent giant Arolla pines – they date back 300 years! The pretty basin dotted with photogenic timber huts was occupied by a vast spread of Austrian tents in 1915–17 and acted as a key sorting and storage point.

Take the main track (n.6) north along Vallon Scuro to **Campo Croce**, marshland fed by meanders of Torrente Boite – according to hearsay, local shepherds purposefully diverted watercourses such as this to curb the impetuous flow and make more drinking water available for their animals. At the junction (1758m), turn left for n.9, a stony track and former wartime mule route. It winds its steady way westward through Arolla pine and larch, levelling out at the 1950m mark to traverse a series of grassy basins dotted with bushes and dwarf mountain pine, the perfect landscape for both shy chamois and marmots. Evidence of the natural phenomenon of karstification is plentiful, with artistic grooved rock surfaces. A puddle-sized lake is passed (**Lago de Fodara**, 1990m) backed by impressive inclined slabs including Lavinores to the south. Not far along is the delightful basin housing a batch of old timber huts with a resident rabbit, not to mention **Rif. Fodara Vedla** (1966m), a particularly comfortable establishment with a lovely view east to the Croda Rossa.

Access to start point:
On the SS 51 8km north of Cortina, where the road curves east towards Landro and Dobbiaco, is the signed turn-off for Rif. Ra Stua and the Parco Naturale Dolomiti d'Ampezzo. The subsequent 3km access road to Rif. Ra Stua is closed to private traffic mid-July to mid-Sept, when a shuttle bus from Fiames via S. Uberto covers the distance. If you can't squeeze into the parking area, leave your vehicle at Fiames, 3km further back. Carless walkers can use the daily SAD bus on the Cortina–Dobbiaco run, then allow an extra 45min one way from S. Uberto (1421m). An alternative to the surfaced road is the slightly longer but delightful 'percorso pedonale' (pedestrian route).

•**Direct exit to
Campo Croce
(45min)**

A matter of minutes east
of Rif. Sennes is the fork
for the straightforward
jeep track (n.7) that
drops southeast via Val
Salata under the line of
cliffs that sweeps down
from the Remeda Rossa
plateau. On the final
stretch to **Campo Croce**
(1758m) is the source of
the River Boite, which
flows past Cortina and
later joins the Piave.

*Rif. Fodara Vedla and the
Croda Rossa*

STAGE TWO: VIA RIF. SENNES (40MIN) TO RIF. BIELLA (1HR)

N.7 for Rif. Sennes starts off as a jeep track. Some 10min
uphill a marked path branches off north through the
shrubs, climbing to a panoramic ridge where the Croda
del Becco (north), Croda Rossa (east) and even the
Cristallo (southeast) come into view. The jeep track is
rejoined the rest of the way to **Rif. Sennes** (2126m),
standing in rather bare surrounds but apparently satisfactory for the herds of hearty cows around.

At this point, should Stage Three look too long and
tiring, make the most of the direct exit route to Campo
Croce.•

In addition to the lane that takes a broad sweep east
then north for Rif. Biella, a more varied and interesting
path (n.6) cuts northeast over a ridge. Leave Rif. Sennes
uphill due north on a rough track, turning off right near a
low shed. You quickly reach undulating terrain with
masses of gentians, edelweiss and marmots, with the
Croda del Becco visible with its trademark shiny grey
inclined slabs. The path drops gradually to join the jeep
track heading east for **Rif. Biella** (2327m), the panorama
ranging southwest to the Tofane and Pelmo.

This is a great hut run by an alpine guide with a life-

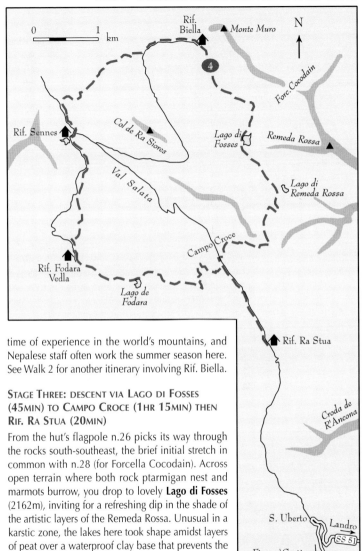

time of experience in the world's mountains, and Nepalese staff often work the summer season here. See Walk 2 for another itinerary involving Rif. Biella.

STAGE THREE: DESCENT VIA LAGO DI FOSSES (45MIN) TO CAMPO CROCE (1HR 15MIN) THEN RIF. RA STUA (20MIN)

From the hut's flagpole n.26 picks its way through the rocks south-southeast, the brief initial stretch in common with n.28 (for Forcella Cocodain). Across open terrain where both rock ptarmigan nest and marmots burrow, you drop to lovely **Lago di Fosses** (2162m), inviting for a refreshing dip in the shade of the artistic layers of the Remeda Rossa. Unusual in a karstic zone, the lakes here took shape amidst layers of peat over a waterproof clay base that prevents the water disappearing underground.

The Cascata di Fanes

Tourist Office Cortina d'Ampezzo tel. 0436-3231/3232

Rif. Biella tel. 0436-866991 CAI, sleeps 45, open 25/6–30/9

Rif. Fodara Vedla tel. 0474-501093 private, sleeps 47, open June–Oct

Rif. Ra Stua tel. 0436-5753 private, sleeps 23, open 15/5–15/10

Rif. Sennes tel. 0474-501092, private, sleeps 62, open 4/6–15/10

Albergo Fiames tel. 0436-2366

Once past the far end of the lake, signposting points you southeast for a brief rise and saddle that provides access to a desolate side valley at the foot of the impressive Piccola Croda Rossa (east). A further lake, **Lago di Remeda Rossa**, is usually dried up. Shortly the clear path cuts down diagonally right (south) into a lovely flowered basin, which leads into dwarf mountain pines and a rough, tiring descent over loose rocks. You eventually emerge on the jeep track at **Campo Croce** (1772m) for the final 20min to **Rif. Ra Stua** (1668m).

5 – The Old Calalzo–Dobbiaco Railway Line

Walking time	4hr 30min
Walk distance	20km/12.4 miles
Difficulty	Grade 1
Map	Tabacco n.03 scale 1:25,000
Start point	Gasthof Drei Zinnen, Landro

Electrified in 1929, the Cortina–Dobbiaco line operated up until the 1960s when bus transport took over. Although track and sleepers were torn up, bridges and station buildings were left standing. The route has since become popular with cross-country skiers and mountain bikers. Walkers too can make the most of this marvellous leisurely piste with changing outlooks onto some impressive Dolomite groups.

The 20km tract of the railway from Lago di Landro south to Cortina is described here. (The 10km Dobbiaco–Landro leg is also feasible, however it tends to stick closer to the road.) A broad track is followed the whole way, and the trifling height gain (120m) and loss (300m) make it suitable even for pushchairs. The former railway track has no waymarking as such, but its linear course is unmistakable. Along the way a string of bus stops can be reached via a short detour, enabling walkers to bail out or slot in at will, and a couple of restaurants and bars are encountered for those who feel the need to treat themselves to a sit-down lunch instead of a scenic picnic. There is plenty of silence and dense wood, and quiet visitors can expect to see both roe deer and chamois.

STAGE ONE: VIA LAGO DI LANDRO (15MIN) THEN CARBONIN (30MIN) TO CIMABANCHE (45MIN)

Gasthof Drei Zinnen (1406m) is purposely set opposite the opening to Valle della Rienza for the stunning view

The Austrian army mapped out the narrow gauge Cortina–Dobbiaco railway line with the imminent war in mind. Work was actually completed by the Italians in 1919 at the conclusion of the conflict, together with the Cortina–Calalzo stretch when the area became part of Italy.

Access to start point:
Gasthof Drei Zinnen stands 1km north of Lago di Landro/Dürrensee and is on the year-round SAD bus line between Cortina and Dobbiaco/Toblach. Those arriving by car will need the SS 51 that runs between Dobbiaco in Val Pusteria south to Cortina and beyond. Drivers are advised to leave their vehicles in the proximity of the hotel at the walk start, rather than the end, and return by bus afterwards, as parking is a rare commodity in the high-flying resort of Cortina, complicated by the convoluted system of one-way streets and pedestrian-only zones.

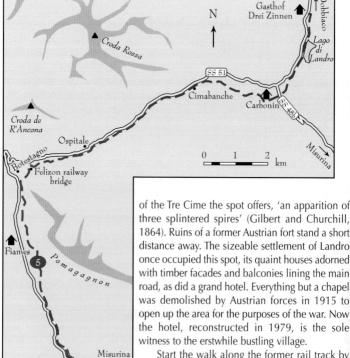

of the Tre Cime the spot offers, 'an apparition of three splintered spires' (Gilbert and Churchill, 1864). Ruins of a former Austrian fort stand a short distance away. The sizeable settlement of Landro once occupied this spot, its quaint houses adorned with timber facades and balconies lining the main road, as did a grand hotel. Everything but a chapel was demolished by Austrian forces in 1915 to open up the area for the purposes of the war. Now the hotel, reconstructed in 1979, is the sole witness to the erstwhile bustling village.

Start the walk along the former rail track by taking the clear lane heading right (south), parallel to the road. **Lago di Landro** (1406m, bus stop) is soon reached, at the base of Monte Piana (explored in Walk 9). The mountain was fiercely contested at length during the First World War. The northern sector was under Austrian control and logically supplied from the lake area by mechanised cableway – an extant wheel has been placed as a memorial nearby. An exposed dizzy route, dubbed the Sentiero dei Pionieri, is also visible, snaking its tortuous way up the western face.

The lake itself is an attractive shallow body of green-white water which has been known to dry up during rainless summers. The track moves along the water's edge, marked by the truncated concrete blocks that once held pylons. After a white gravel bed of a watercourse, it goes off into mixed wood, heading in the direction of the impressive Cristallo massif.

As the track crosses the road to Misurina, you leave the realms of the Sesto Nature Park and pass close to **Carbonin** (1437m, bus stop). These days it consists solely of the upmarket Hotel Ploner, in contrast to the former popular summer retreat which hosted figures such as Gustav Mahler. The hotel had a modest start as an inn opened in 1836 by the Ploner family to cater to the needs of timber hauliers, while the name Carbonin came from the numerous charcoal burners in the proximity. It soon became a jumping-off point for mountaineers and walkers, and consequently a meeting place for guides, such as famous Michael Innerkofler. Anna Ploner, on the other hand, was the first woman to scale the Tre Cime.

As the track proceeds west now, the Croda Rossa can be seen (west-northwest). **Cimabanche** (1530m, bus stop) and its old station mark the end of the gentle climb, as it is a strategic watershed between the two river systems. It also marked the Austrian–Italian front, now transformed into the demarcation between the German-speaking province of Bolzano and the Italian province of Belluno. However, of more immediate interest will inevitably be the tempting aroma of barbecued meat wafting from the outdoor café that is hard to resist.

STAGE TWO: TO OSPITALE (1HR), FIAMES (1HR) THEN CORTINA (1HR)

From here on the route is a gentle descent below the Croda de R'Ancona, with fleeting glimpses of the Tofane through the trees from time to time. The track now runs past a couple of lakes featuring wild ducks and through meadows, parallel to the road as far as **Ospitale** (1490m, bus stop). This is the site of a 13th-century frescoed chapel and hospice for pilgrims, damaged in the war years but since carefully reconstructed and transformed into an atmospheric restaurant.

Then far away from traffic once more, there are views west to Monte Vallon Bianco and Fanes. Keep your eyes

Landro and its lake seen from M. Piana

skinned for chamois on the opposite bank – the steep scrubby rock terrain is their playground. After a short section of tunnel you bear south and the Austrian wartime **Felizon rail bridge** comes into view. Quite a piece of history with its criss-cross struts, the covered lattice structure occupies an impressive position straddling jagged cliffs 70m above a tortuous torrent bed. According to legend, the chasm was once inhabited by a mysterious mother and son; clad in green, they were known to sleep with the cascading water as their blanket and a moss-covered rock for a pillow.

(An even more dramatic footbridge is located a short distance downhill, beneath the towering buttress of Botestagno, site of the meagre ruins of a strategic medieval castle controlled by Aquileia, Venice or Austria, depending on the period in history.)

Next is a long, dark and often muddy tunnel which protected the train line from avalanches; it is better avoided by taking the path detouring right if the electric lighting happens to be off. The milky blue of the Torrente Boite comes into sight, backed by the rear of Col Rosa then the Tofane. Vast swathes of dwarf mountain pine interrupted by vast flows of scree and rubble from rock-slides are traversed under the towering west flanks of the Pomagagnon, with marvellous shades of pink-red and grey-cream.

Not far along and you'll be above **Fiames** (1293m, bus stop), a cluster of buildings. With a good 1h to go, continue on past another former railway station (drinking water) and through the larch wood before the residential zone and **Cortina** (1210m). The route emerges at the bus terminal, the premises easily recognisable as the former railway station.

Return to Lago di Landro and your vehicle by bus.

Tourist Office Cortina d'Ampezzo tel. 0436-3231/3232

Albergo Fiames tel. 0436-2366

Gasthof Dre Zinnen (Landro) tel. 0474-972633

Hotel Ploner (Carbonin) tel. 0474-977111

6 – Sesto Dolomites: Croda Rossa di Sesto Traverse

Walking time	2hr 45min (2hr if Castelliere is avoided)
Walk distance	6.5km/3.9 miles
Difficulty	Grade 2 (Grade 1 if Castelliere is avoided)
Ascent/descent	600m/300m (400m/100m if Castelliere is avoided)
Map	Tabacco n.010 scale 1:25,000
Start point	Passo M. Croce Comelico

The pass where the walk starts marks the former border between Italy and the Austro-Hungarian Empire, transformed into what is now the line between the German-speaking South Tyrol and Italian-speaking Veneto regions of Italy as from 1918. Scattered constructions dating back to the conflict are encountered.

STAGE ONE: ASCENT TO THE CASTELLIERE FORK (1HR 10MIN)

From the ample grassy road pass of **Passo M. Croce Comelico** (1630m), path n.15a sets off southwest on a rough wide track behind the hotel. Rather monotonous at first, it passes below a ski lift in the proximity of a fort dating back to the World War One hostilities, then enters pretty mixed conifer wood. The climb is easy and gradual, often amongst huge boulders, and the path quickly reaches the dazzling flanks of the Croda Sora i Colesei/Arzalpenkopf, the area dotted with bunkers. Some 40min from the pass is a **junction at 1925m** (where n.124 proceeds southeast for Rif. Berti) and you keep right (west). Mostly on a level now amongst shrub vegetation well above the conifers, the route crosses a vast basin and then a river of scree over a minor

This delightful gentle walk in the north-eastern Sesto Dolomites, close to the Austrian border, is especially popular with German-speaking visitors. An initial easy climb leads to a marvellous panoramic traverse, which concludes at the renowned high altitude Prati di Croda Rossa/ Rotwandwiesen meadows below the magnificent Croda Rossa di Sesto/Sextener Rotwand dominating the eastern extremity of the Val Pusteria/ Pustertal. The ensuing descent is by leisurely gondola car. The only 'difficulty' entailed in the walk is the steep, rough 100m descent from the Castelliere/ Burgstall viewpoint, but an alternative shorter and more straightforward lower path can be followed.

Access to start point:
as this is a traverse, unless you have two cars and leave one at the start and finish points, you'll need to catch the SAD bus (June–late Sept) from Sesto/Sexten in Val Pusteria via the SS 52 to Passo M. Croce Comelico/Kreuzbergpass. The Saita bus company also has a year-round service via S. Stefano di Cadore, then the pass and Val Pusteria.

The Kabinenbahn Rotwand gondola lift to and from Bagni di Moso operates early June to early Oct, and the SAD bus to the pass makes a stop at the downhill station.

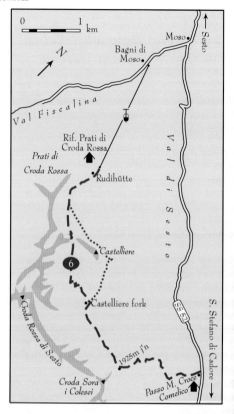

watercourse. The next landmark is the **Castelliere fork**, where there are two possibilities.

Lower Castelliere path (30min)
Keep right for the easy route, which means sticking to the straightforward and wider n.15a to circle the base of the Castelliere outcrop, essentially on a level. About half an hour around in light wood, you rejoin the following route, just above the Prati di Croda Rossa, cutting about 45min off the total timing.

STAGE TWO: CLIMB TO CASTELLIERE (40MIN) THEN DESCENT TO PRATI DI CRODA ROSSA (45MIN)

From the above fork, the more scenic (if marginally more difficult) route n.15b breaks off left for the 300m climb. At first it follows the edge of a rubble flow, often harbouring old snow right through the summer. The climb is relentless, and it takes you up close to some sheer cliffs with a series of First World War trenches at their base. (A path breaks off south here for the Croda Rossa di Sesto peak – experienced climbers only.) The name **Castelliere** may be a reference to a prehistoric fortified settlement, as the promontory certainly occupies a dominating position. The flowery saddle (2235m) means a plunging scenario down to the Prati di Croda Rossa meadows and huts virtually at your feet. On a Sunday afternoon in summer, the stirring strains of the local Tyrolean style band waft up, and you might even hear the odd yodel.

The path moves left briefly with an overhanging passage, and First World War positions are visible overhead. Now comes the plunge via a gully choked with loose rubble, necessitating a firm tread. After 20min in descent the gradient eases off somewhat and the terrain is anchored by alpenrose, larch and mountain avens. The alternative 15a joins up, and you reach the upper edge of the meadows. The bustling restaurant **Rudihütte**, where much merrymaking takes place, is en route to the gondola lift, whilst a second hut, **Rif. Prati di Croda Rossa/ Rotwandwiesehütte**, with panoramic guesthouse style accommodation, is on a signposted branch to the left. This elevated basin-cum-platform, known as the meadows **Prati di Croda Rossa** (1900m), offers great views of the immense Croda Rossa di Sesto, whose flanks you have been skirting for the last couple of hours, in addition to the Tre Scarperi/Dreischuster group due west, and the darker ridges, with M. Elmo/Helm to the north over Val Pusteria.

STAGE THREE: GONDOLA CAR DESCENT TO BAGNI DI MOSO (10MIN)

The gondola lift will transport you down to **Bagni di Moso** (1362m) in a matter of minutes, whereas you'll need a good hour on foot on path n.15/151.

Tourist Office
Sesto/Sexten
tel. 0474-710310

Albergo Passo Monte
Croce
tel. 0474-710328

Rif. Prati di Croda
Rossa/
Rotwandwiesehütte
tel. 0474-710651
private, sleeps 25, open
June–Oct

Some of the most breathtaking scenery in the Dolomites is accessible to walkers who embark on this superb round-trip in the wonderful Sesto group, not far south of the Austrian border. Enclosed in a 116km² nature park, the scenery ranges from meadows thick with wild flowers and picturesque alpine tarns to ever-changing scenes of rock pinnacles, soaring peaks and vast scree slopes brightened by gay alpine blooms. In contrast, during the terrible 1915–18 war a front line cut across the articulated mountain range which was contested between the crumbling Austrian-Hapsburg Empire and the young Italian nation. Lines of protected trenches snaked their way along dividing ridges and up the highest peaks, held by special alpine troops, and widespread evidence throughout the high areas remains as testimony to this period.

7 – Sesto Dolomites: the Val Fiscalina Tour

Walking time	6hr (shorter variants given below)
Walk distance	17km/10.5 miles
Difficulty	Grade 2
Ascent/descent	1225m/1225m
Map	Tabacco n.010 scale 1:25,000
Start point	Dolomitenhof, Val Fiscalina

There's something for everyone here, as attested by the high visitor numbers. A string of high-altitude huts is encountered en route, each manned for the entire summer period, which provides handy points for meals and, of course, emergencies.

As described here the tour is long, tiring and average in terms of difficulty, though eminently rewarding. It can, however, easily be split into two wonderful and more straightforward routes: either take Stage One south as far as Rif. Zsigmondy-Comici (770m height gain/loss, 4hr return timing), or climb the southwestern branch to Rif. Locatelli (950m height gain/loss, 4hr 30min return timing), returning the same way in both cases.

Stage One: via Rif. Fondo Valle (20min) to Rif. Zsigmondy-Comici (1hr 50min)

From the **Dolomitenhof** (1454m), where a handy board lists the valley's huts and whether or not they are open, the easy level track (n.102/103) heads due south at the foot of the mammoth Tre Scarperi group (west), whose shark teeth points rise to 3145m, the highest in the park. Opposite are the outliers of the Croda Rossa di Sesto. You can always rattle along this stretch in a jingling horse-drawn cart should you feel the urge.

As you approach **Rif. Fondo Valle** (1548m), the layout of the mountains dubbed the 'Sesto sun dial' (they are akin to a clock face) becomes clear: southeast is Cima Dieci (peak at 'ten o'clock'), better known as the Croda Rossa di Sesto, then south-southeast stands Cima Undici (eleven), due south naturally is Cima Dodici (twelve), also known as Croda dei Toni, while Cima Una (one) over-shadows the hut to the south-southwest.

Plough straight ahead on what quickly becomes a path across bleached gravel terrain anchored down by spreading dwarf mountain pines for the strategic fork at the opening of Val Sassovecchio, where the main routes separate at a pictorial signboard: go left on n.103 to ascend Val Fiscalina Alta. The climb along the eastern flank of Cima Una is relentless, though distractions come in the form of alpenrose and the marvellous views that continue to improve. Zigzags take the sting out of the steepest final sections to **Rif. Zsigmondy-Comici** (2224m), where you can collapse on the wonderful terrace.

The hut was named after two leading figures in moun-taineering: the first an outstanding member of the Austrian Alpine Club that ideated the construction in the 1880s, and the second a pioneer Italian climber from the 1940s. East across the valley below M. Popera a horizontal ledge can be seen: during the First World War it was hewn out of the rock face then painstakingly fitted with cables by the intrepid Italian forces, and came to be known as the Strada degli Alpini. A popular aided route nowadays, it requires experience and equipment, though you can always purchase one of the incredible postcard scenes!

STAGE TWO: VIA RIF. PIAN DI CENGIA (1HR) TO RIF LOCATELLI (1HR)

A further 300m climb is next on the agenda as path n.101 follows a winding wartime route west. Meagre patches of grass, and even hardy members of the daisy family, are interspersed with stone and scattered war remains on the approach to the col, **Passo Fiscalino** (2519m). A front ran through here during the hostilities, as testified by the trenches and sentry lookouts, chilling reminders of the practicalities of high-altitude conflict. If you don't mind heights and are sure-footed, take the time to explore the passageways.

Access to start point:
Car-bound visitors will need to branch off the SS 52 a few km southwest of Sesto/Sexten for the southbound Val Fiscalina/Fischleintal. The road is closed to traffic in the vicinity of the Dolomitenhof hotel and bus stop, and there's a car park that charges hefty fees.

Others will need to catch the daily Holzer bus that runs from Sesto via Moso to the Dolomitenhof, mid-June through to mid-Oct.

Leaving the Croda dei Toni behind you, keep right along the ample ledge for nearby **Rif. Pian di Cengia** (2528m). Tucked into a sheltering rock alcove, the tiny immaculate hut serves delicious hearty soups that go a long way to warming walkers in the windy chill that seems to prevail here.

Forcella Pian di Cengia (2522m) is the next landmark, a mere cut in the rock crest and leading into an immense scree-filled amphitheatre littered with more war material in the shape of timbers and barbed wire from fortified positions. You drop abruptly north via a barren gully to start with, then the path levels out for the panoramic traverse west, the stark surrounds enlivened by delicate yellow Rhaetian poppies and lilac round-leafed penny cress. Below lies a sparkling tarn, emerald or sky blue in colour, depending on the weather. The final section crosses welcome grassy terrain below M. Paterno and the 'sausage' (Frankfurter

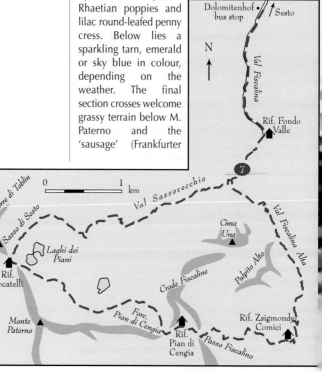

Rif. Zsigmondy-Comici opposite M. Popera with the Strada degli Alpini

Wurstel), and above a pretty cluster of lakes, the Laghi dei Piani. **Rif. Locatelli** (2405m) at Forcella di Toblin, must be the best-visited hut in the whole of the Dolomites for its amazing position opposite the spectacular world famous Tre Cime, whose sheer sides rise solemnly to the south from an immense base of scree, and take on beautiful hues of pink and orange at sunset. The hut is also covered in Walk 8, including a side trip to Sasso di Sesto, the prominent isolated mount at its rear.

Stage Three: descent to Rif. Fondo Valle (1hr 30min) and Dolomitenhof (20min)

It's all downhill from **Rif. Locatelli** eastwards on path n.102. The former pasture basin Alpe dei Piani, with the lakes, is traversed before things become relatively steeper and timber crossbars reinforce the path and help minimise the erosion caused by the thousands of boots that tread the route. You are soon in Val Sassovecchio, bordered by the impressive Crode Fiscaline and Cima Una to its south and the northern sector of the Tre

Overlooking Laghi dei Piani after an October snowfall

Tourist Office
Sesto/Sexten
tel. 0474-710310

Rif. Fondo
Valle/Talschlußhütte
tel. 0474-710606
private, sleeps 20, open
June to mid-Oct

Rif. A. Locatelli
tel. 0474-972002 CAI,
sleeps 180,
open 20/6–30/9

Rif. Pian di
Cengia/Büllelejochhütte
tel. 337-451517
private, sleeps 11, open
15/6 to early Oct

Rif. Zsigmondy-Comici
tel. 0474-710358 CAI,
sleeps 77,
open 15/6–7/10

Scarperi group to the north. The path sticks close to the watercourse, usually a meagre affair, the odd tree appearing now above the scrubby shrubs. Keep left at the n.102/n.103 junction for the short shady stretch to **Rif. Fondo Valle** (1548m) then **Dolomitenhof** (1454m), with the bus stop and car park once again.

8 – Sesto Dolomites: Tre Cime di Lavaredo Circuit

Walking time	3hr 30min + 40min for optional Sasso di Sesto
Walk distance	10km/6 miles
Difficulty	Grade 1–2
Ascent/descent	340m/340m
Map	Tabacco n.010 scale 1:25,000
Start point	Rif. Auronzo

One of the most photographed land-marks of the Dolomites is the awesome Tre Cime di Lavaredo (or Drei Zinnen), likened to 'Egyptian Colossi' by Gilbert and Churchill (1864). Peaking at 2999m with the Cima Grande, they were not successfully scaled until 1896 by Paul Grohmann. An enduring magnet for ambitious climbers attracted by the magnif-icent sheer faces which turn pastel pinks and all but flame red towards sundown, they are easily visited at close quarters by walkers.

The Sesto group that encompasses the Tre Cime di Lavaredo is practically bisected by the administrative border between Italy's German-speaking South Tyrol and the predominantly Italian Veneto region, which was the frontier between Hapsburg Austria and Italy until 1918. The entire range was involved in the First World War, and wherever you turn are trench systems gouged by hand out of the rough dolomite surface, defensive barricades of stones heaped up by platoons of soldiers and the ubiq-uitous barbed wire.

One wonderful way to appreciate the Tre Cime formation in summer is by a pedestrian circumnaviga-tion, during which their unusual shapes mutate from sharp points to soft corners, the three sections apparently merging into one. They are separated by profound gashes caused by erosion along ancient fault lines dating back to the era when the rock was underground. Good paths lead all the way round on open terrain with views spacing in all directions, thus making a highly spectacular walk.

A word on the area's popularity and access: the walk's start point, Rif. Auronzo, stands at the head of a toll road that climbs in a dramatic series of switchback bends from Misurina on the southern side. Owned and managed by the Auronzo Council, it is a bone of contention between the council and mountain lovers and

At Forcella Lavaredo after an early autumn snowfall

environmentalists due to the excessive amount of traffic that the council allows (at a high price) to circulate and park at the foot of the Tre Cime, and the apparently unchecked expansion of unsightly giant parking areas. Proposals for alternatives include a funicular-type railway. In the meantime the bus can be used. Quieter access from the north is feasible – a trek of several hours' duration from Val Fiscalina (see Walk 7).

With the exception of the area around Rif. Auronzo and the car parks, extremely busy all summer, the usual rule applies – the further you walk away from the road, the quieter it gets. Take your own drink and food unless you plan on queuing up with the multitudes at the three *rifugi* en route, and remember that you're at a fairly high altitude and should always carry protective clothing.

Access to start point:
Rif. Auronzo, 7km north of Misurina, is the destination of the Tre Cime bus line from Cortina (Dolomiti Bus, July to mid-Sept) as well as the SAD service from Dobbiaco/Toblach in Val Pusteria/Pustertal (3rd week June to mid-Sept).

By car for Misurina take the SS 48 from Cortina or Auronzo, otherwise the SS 48b from Carbonin/Schluderbach in Val di Landro/Höhlensteintal. Then you need the minor road north signed for the Tre Cime di Lavaredo/Drei Zinnen and Rif. Auronzo. The toll booth is a few km up, just after Lago d'Antorno.

STAGE ONE: VIA FORCELLA LAVAREDO (30MIN) THEN RIF. LOCATELLI (45MIN)

From **Rif. Auronzo** (2320m) and its chaos, head east along the wide, level former military track n.101, beneath the dizzy threesome of the Tre Cime. Soon after a commemorative chapel for the alpine forces who lost their lives in these inhospitable realms during the First World War, the track curves north. Backed by Croda Passaporto is **Rif. Lavaredo** (2344m) on a vast stony platform.

Leave the track now for the clear path n.101 that branches off left (north) to climb to **Forcella Lavaredo** (2454m), where a breathtaking panorama opens up: apart from the side views onto the regular blocks of the Tre Cime which defy description, right (north-northeast) is M. Paterno, then the northern line-up taking in the Tre Scarperi and Baranci groups, while to the south behind you are the crazy pointed Cadini spires. This saddle was an important Italian position during the hostilities, and it was from here that Rif. Locatelli was shelled and burnt down in 1915.

Path n.101 continues in the same direction, dipping slightly below the ridge of M. Paterno, riddled with wartime galleries, before a lovely level traverse across the dramatic scree slope. A slight climb up an outcrop brings you out at **Rif. Locatelli** (2405m), located at Forcella di Toblin, a stunning spot for admiring the Tre Cime. First opened in 1883 at the cost of 813 florins, the hut needed extensions soon afterwards as visitor numbers

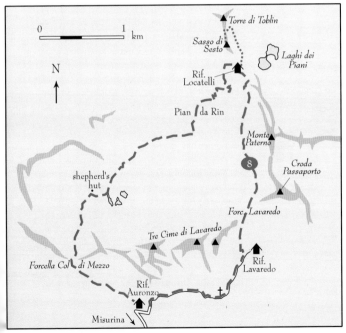

in the following seven-year period shot up to 3375. The figure would barely cover a matter of days now in midsummer!

A recommended side trip follows to Sasso di Sesto, fiercely contested during the First World War.

Side trip to Sasso di Sesto (40min return)

Right behind the hut (northwest) is the Sasso di Sesto, its base pierced by a line of man-made rock windows. A signed path for the Via Ferrata Torre di Toblin can be found near Rif Locatelli's chapel. Follow this up to the saddle that separates the Torre di Toblin from the Sasso di Sesto, and turn sharp left (south) for the nearby 2539m top (20min), an extraordinary lookout that even takes in the far-off Marmolada southwest, preceded by the Tofane and the Cristallo. Return to Rif. Locatelli the same way.

Stage Two: via Forcella Col di Mezzo (1hr 50min) and return to Rif. Auronzo (25min)

From **Rif. Locatelli** take n.102 west in common with the descent to Landro and make sure that after about a quarter of an hour of ample curves downhill you fork off southwest on n.105. It traverses a lovely undulating basin (**Pian da Rin**) that is sparsely grassed and hosts a colony of shy marmots. This glorious route is much quieter than the outward path and gives you plenty of time to appreciate the colossal peaks ahead. Early summer visitors may encounter old patches of snow in the hollows; however, whatever the season it's important to keep track of the irregular red/white paint splashes marking the route as landmarks are rare. One useful point is a deserted stone **shepherd's hut** (2283m), an evocative rest point. Then it's a steady easy ascent to **Forcella Col di Mezzo** (2315m), also spelt del Col de Mezo, which marks the return to the south side of the Tre Cime, with more wonderful views over the Cadini, Sorapiss and the Marmarole range. N.105 continues southeast for the final strolling stretch back to **Rif. Auronzo** (2320m) and the car park.

Tourist Office Misurina tel. 0435-39016

Rif. Auronzo tel. 0435-39002 CAI, sleeps 125, open 1/6–8/10

Rif. Lavaredo tel. 0436-39135 private, sleeps 30, open 1/6–30/9

Rif. A. Locatelli tel. 0474-972002 CAI, sleeps 180, open 20/6–30/9

9 – Sesto Dolomites: Monte Piana

Walking time	4hr 20min (less 1hr with jeep taxi to Rif. Bosi)
Walk distance	14km/8.5 miles
Difficulty	Grade 1 (2–3 Stage Three descent)
Ascent/descent	600m/600m
Map	Tabacco n.010 or n.03 scale 1:25,000
Start point	Lago d'Antorno

Only 12km from Val Pusteria, the heart of South Tyrol defence during the 1915–17 hostilities, stands Monte Piana, a flat-topped, oversized hill. An Italian military access road is clearly visible climbing the south side in wide zigzags from what is now the resort of Misurina and its picturesque lake. M. Piana, literally 'flat mount', now refers to the whole of this humble rounded mountain, whereas during the First World War the northernmost part, referred to as M. Piano, was an Austrian stronghold linked by two difficult paths exposed to enemy fire and a mechanised cableway to Lago di Landro, while southern M. Piana was Italian, supplied from Misurina and a purpose-built mule track from Val Rinbianco. The drawn-out hostilities caused shocking loss of life, and the entire mountain top is honeycombed with trench systems, artillery positions, fortifications and tunnels. Especially fierce fighting took place during the summer of 1915 – Italian losses alone totalled 833 in a mere five days in July – and there were further losses during the terrible winters and devastating snow storms. The Italian contingents rapidly abandoned the mountain in summer 1917, when reinforcements were urgently needed on the Isonzo front to the east, where Austro-German forces eventually broke through.

'The Italians have justly baptised this mountain "Monte Pianto" [Mountain of Tears]. It has already cost our side and the Italians so much blood and will cost even more, that I do not know if its possession can justify such a great sacrifice… So many have been buried here! So many corpses alongside the trenches! I'm not the one to say if this was really necessary; I only know that this is what was wanted by those in the rear, with their peremptory orders. In any case that's not my concern; my task is to obey.' (Austrian army captain, First World War)

SHORTER WALKS IN THE DOLOMITES

Well before the conflict, M. Piana was traversed by the border between the Republic of Venice and Austria, and a series of original granite marker stones dating back to 1753 are dotted over the plateau.

The fascinating round-trip described here follows a straightforward clear route, accessible to all and very rewarding. The marvellous 360° panorama from the top of M. Piana is enormously helpful in putting the mountains of the Eastern Dolomites into perspective.

Access to start point:

The start point, Lago d'Antorno, 2km above Misurina, is on the Tre Cime bus line from Cortina (Dolomiti Bus, July to mid-Sept) as well as the SAD service from Dobbiaco/Toblach in Val Pusteria/Pustertal (3rd week June to mid-Sept).

By car for Misurina take the SS 48 from Cortina or Auronzo, otherwise the SS 48b from Carbonin/ Schluderbach in Val di Landro/Höhlensteintal. Then you need the road for the Tre Cime di Lavaredo and Rif. Auronzo. There is ample parking at the lakeside.

As an alternative to the climb in Stage One, Rif. Bosi is now served by a jeep shuttle service (mid-June–start of Oct) which departs from Bar Genzianella, around the corner from Misurina. The narrow road, mostly surfaced, is closed to non-authorised traffic.

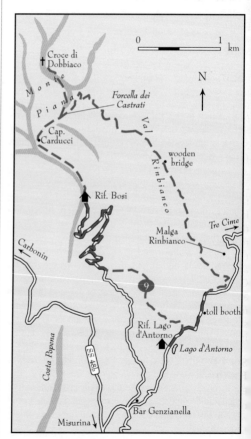

Reasonable height gain and loss are entailed in the walk, however a jeep taxi can be used as far as Rif. Bosi if desired. **Note:** the descent in Stage Four begins with a brief exposed tract, followed by a narrow path which is a little rough going at first, but nothing problematic in good conditions.

In the late 1970s an Austrian group, Dolomiten-freunde, together with volunteers from all over Europe, set about restoring many of the war remains on M. Piana, creating what amounts to an open-air museum – so allow plenty of extra time for exploring. They also mapped out a comprehensive *sentiero storico* (historical route). Marked as 6a with yellow and black signposting, it takes a couple of hours to complete and involves a number of exposed and difficult sections along cliff edges, some fitted with cables. It serves as a suitable extension to the walk described here for those with experience and a head for heights.

STAGE ONE: FROM LAGO D'ANTORNO TO RIF. BOSI (1HR 15MIN)

A matter of minutes up the road from **Lago d'Antorno** (1866m) a signed path for Rif. Bosi forks off left into the trees. It climbs easily through a wood of sweet conifers interspersed with pretty heather, trumpet gentians and dwarf alpenrose. At about 1900m you join the panoramic road that started out from Bar Genzianella, and soon encounter the odd short cut. The easy gradient gives ample time for appreciating the changing aspect of the Cristallo Group to the southwest, the Cadini (southeast) and the Tre Cime (east-northeast). A path cuts the final road curve, but be warned – it's steep. Then at 2205m stands **Rif. Bosi**, named after a young Italian captain. An interesting museum pertaining to the war adjoins the hut.

STAGE TWO: VIA CAPANNA CARDUCCI (20MIN) TO FORCELLA DEI CASTRATI (15MIN)

Facing **Rif. Bosi**, take the path left across the grassy slopes of the wind-swept plateau, totally devoid of tree cover here. An easy climb past a string of wartime positions leads to the **Capanna Carducci** hut and pyramidal monu-

At the Italian stronghold on M. Piana, with Picco di Vallandro and Austria in the background

ment at 2325m, so-named after a visit by the famous Italian poet and Nobel prize winner Giosuè Carducci. There are simply wonderful views, ranging from the unmistakable blood-red Croda Rossa directly west to Cristallo in the southwest, Cadini to the southeast and the towering Tre Cime peaks to the east. There are also a lot of First World War constructions to be seen, as this was a former Italian stronghold. Moreover, from this point the configuration of the mountain as a whole becomes clear: note its isolated position and two rounded, exposed promontories linked by a narrow neck of land, Forcella dei Castrati, no-man's land for a long time. The signpost for the route to Carbonin refers to one of the Austrian wartime supply routes.

From **Capanna Carducci** head north-northeast for the shallow earth depression at 2272m, **Forcella dei Castrati**.

STAGE THREE: TO CROCE DI DOBBIACO (30MIN RETURN TIME)

Before descending from M. Piana, an extension to the northernmost former Austrian-held zone is warmly recommended. A clear path proceeds via a concentration of fortified positions and excavated constructions, including points marking the Italian tunnels which undermined a good part of the plateau. At a remarkable dizzy lookout directly over Val di Landro stands the massive wooden cross **Croce di Dobbiaco**/Toblach Kreuz

(2305m). The rock base here has undergone extensive karstification so watch your step amidst the cracks and crevices. In the proximity is a military cemetery as well as one of the original mid-18th-century Venetian border stones, though your attention will more likely be drawn by the surrounding mountains: the Baranci and Tre Scarperi groups are at close quarters, to the north and northwest respectively. Make your way back to **Forcella dei Castrati**.

STAGE FOUR: DESCENT TO VAL RINBIANCO (1HR) THEN RETURN TO LAGO D'ANTORNO (1HR)

From **Forcella dei Castrati** take the narrow path n.6a in descent to the left, marked for Val Castrati and the 'Gallerie delle mine'. A fascinating route, its exposed stretches equipped with a guiding cable, it follows a natural ledge past man-made caverns and entrances to the Italian tunnels intended for mines but never put to use. As the abundant piles of droppings suggest, this is a favourite haunt of chamois, while marmots inhabit the rubble-strewn basin below. After 15min the path widens and a junction is reached – keep right for Val Rinbianco via the erstwhile mule track for Italian supplies. Tight zigzags lead past more tunnels and down to a fork (right) for a variant from Rif. Bosi, which you ignore. The going is easier now, though springy dwarf mountain pines threaten to encroach from all sides. A series of clearings with ruined barracks is traversed, then a rocky gully. At last the path emerges at a rickety **wooden bridge** over an alpine brook in **Val Rinbianco** (1718m).

Take the right branch of n.108/111 between the rocky flanks of M. Piana and Croda dell'Anghena to the left. Some 45min and hordes of grazing cows later, you pass below summer farm Malga Rinbianco. The path curves right across a watercourse and climbs to join the Tre Cime road near the toll booth. Turn right for the 10min stretch back to **Lago d'Antorno** and the warm atmosphere of its restaurant/guesthouse, Rif. Lago Antorno.

Tourist Office Misurina
tel. 0435-39016

Rif. Bosi
tel. 0435-39034
private, sleeps 15, open
mid-June–start of Oct

Rif. Lago Antorno
tel. 0435-39148
private, sleeps 30,
open 10/6–20/10

The marvellous Cadini di Misurina are an awe-inspiring series of jagged crests, slender spires and massive towers dissected by vast abrupt valleys and cirques – the actual *cadin* or *ciadin*, though the term has been extended to the mountains themselves. A relatively compact group whose crazy shapes and stunning host of peaks rise from a pedestal of dark green forest and pastures, it is often reflected in the picturesque deep blue-green Misurina lake. It is also a close neighbour of the renowned Tre Cime di Lavaredo/Drei Zinnen group which draws great crowds, though the Cadini fortunately are rarely busy. The group is a playground for climbers on the *vie ferrate* aided routes, though a number of excellent paths also lead non-experts into the magical inner realms.

10 – Cadini di Misurina Loop

Walking time	2hr 45min
Walk distance	8km/4.9 miles
Difficulty	Grade 2 (short aided stretch Grade 3)
Ascent/descent	550m/550m
Map	Tabacco n.010 scale 1:25,000
Start point	Lago d'Antorno

The itinerary described is straightforward, with the exception of a descent down a rock face at the beginning of Stage Two, aided by fixed cable. It is not particularly exposed, and as it follows immediately on from Rif. Fonda Savio it can be avoided by simply turning back and returning via the ascent route. Remember that the sheltered valleys retain snow well into the summer.

On the other hand, as an extension to the route described here, those with some climbing experience and a head for heights can embark on the Sentiero Bonacossa, the rewarding partially aided traverse from Rif. Fonda Savio all the way to Rif. Auronzo, which follows pathways, ledges and climbs prepared by the Italian Alpine Corps 1915–16. The initial section is followed in the itinerary below, however it is the Forcella Rinbianco to Rif. Auronzo section that becomes interesting, involving exposed lengths and some climbing – allow a good 1hr 30min in good conditions for this final leg. A summer bus will drop you back at the start of the walk afterwards.

STAGE ONE: TO RIF. FONDA SAVIO (1HR 15MIN)

A short distance downhill from **Lago d'Antorno** (1866m), at the start of the **dirt track** which is part of path n.115 (1800m), Rif. Fonda Savio is visible due west at the head of the immense valley. Only 10min up through thick wood is the loading point for the refuge's mechanised cableway at **Pian dei Spiriti** (1896m). Here a clear path takes over for the steady winding climb up the flowered flanks of Col dei Tocci. Views back west are dominated by M. Cristallo, whereas northwest is M. Piana. At about 2100m you enter the vast scree valley of **Ciadin dei Tocci**, a magnificent amphitheatre surrounded by soaring peaks such as Punta dei Spiriti and Cima d'Antorno (south). Above the tree line now, there are masses of colourful wild flowers, with the likes of Rhaetian poppies, pink thrift and mountain avens along the path, though your attention will probably be on the Torre Wundt, to the left of the refuge, as it is usually swarming with climbers. A set of wooden stairs leads up to the rock platform and commanding position of **Rif. Fonda Savio** (2367m, 1hr 15min from the road). It is dominated to the south by the slender Torre Alvise and the Castello Incantato which precedes the Cima Cadin Nord-Ovest. The refuge was built in 1963 by the Trieste branch of the Alpine Club in memory of three brothers who lost their lives during the Second World War, and is one of those exemplary, spotlessly clean huts run along traditional lines.

Access to start point:
See Walk 9 for Lago d'Antorno – bus passengers should then walk back downhill a couple of minutes for the signed track where the walk starts.

For drivers, there is parking both at the track for Rif. Fonda Savio (1.5km from Misurina) and at nearby Lago d'Antorno.

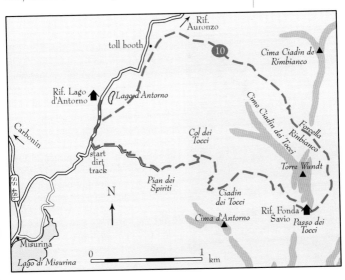

Tourist Office Misurina
tel. 0435-39016

Rif. Fonda Savio tel.
0435-39036 CAI,
sleeps 40, open late
June–start of Oct

Rif. Lago Antorno tel.
0435-39148 private,
sleeps 30, open
10/6–20/10

*Rif. Fonda Savio with
Torre Winkler*

Stage Two: via Forcella Rinbianco (30min) to Lago d'Antorno (1hr)

Close to the refuge is **Passo dei Tocci**, with a breathtaking line-up of peaks and spires dominating the innermost Vallon del Nevaio, starting due south with Cima Eotvös, Cima Cadin di San Lucano and Cimon di Croda Liscia, to mention but a few. This is the start of n.117 – the Sentiero Bonacossa. To drop northeast into the valley, follow the cable carefully down the steep rock flank, a matter of 10min under good conditions, with a few hands-on stretches. Once down, stick to the path straight ahead, past the junction where n.112 branches off right, and proceed north along the desolate Vallon del Nevaio where, as the name suggests, snow persists well into summer, covering the chaos of fallen rocks. The towering Tre Cime come into sight north, while the Torre Wundt cannot be missed up left. **Forcella Rinbianco** (2176m) is easily reached, just below a series of First World War fortifications. (To continue on to Rif. Auronzo, keep to n.117 at this point.)

Path n.119 leads easily westwards down the Ciadin de Rinbianco, with excellent views of M. Piana and its zigzagging military tracks. A cluster of massive fallen boulders is passed beneath the Cime Ciadin dei Tocci, before a gully followed by light wood and pasture. Keep left at a dirt track (signed n.101 for Rif. Auronzo). The Tre Cime are even more majestic from this angle. About 45min from the pass will see you close to the booth for the toll road. The choice here is either to follow the asphalt left to **Lago d'Antorno** (1886m) and its welcoming refuge or to bear left just before the road for a faint unmarked path; this cuts south through a clearing and wood behind the lake to emerge on the tarmac a short way uphill from the **dirt track** at the start of the walk.

11 – Sorapiss: Rif. Vandelli Traverse

Walking time	4hr 30min (3hr 30min if limited to Rif. Vandelli)
Walk distance	12.5km/7.8 miles
Difficulty	Grade 2–3 (Grade 1–2 to Rif. Vandelli)
Ascent/descent	750m/750m (250m/250m if limited to Rif. Vandelli)
Map	Tabacco n.03 scale 1:25,000
Start point	Passo Tre Croci

Unlike the rugged rocky heart of the Sorapiss which soars to 3205m, dominating the resort township of Cortina, luckily the northernmost edge of the group is accessible to the average walker. This varied loop route leads to a lovely hut set below towering Punta Sorapiss, and guarantees extensive views over neighbouring Dolomites, combined with good chances of spotting wild chamois mountain goats.

The chequered history of Rif. Vandelli itself warrants a few lines. Recently the object of a bitter property dispute, it has suffered devastation at the hand of avalanches, rock slides and fire on numerous occasions since its inauguration in 1891 by the Alpine Club in this former Austrian territory. Nowadays managed by the Venice branch, it makes for a handy panoramic lunch stop; however, be warned that the hut can get extremely busy, especially on August weekends. The water at the *rifugio* is classified unsuitable for drinking purposes, so either carry your own or be prepared to purchase the bottled mineral variety.

The walk can easily be simplified if you limit yourself to Stage One as far as Rif. Vandelli, a very rewarding route in itself, then return to the road pass the same way.

The dialect name Sorapiss literally means 'above the waterfall'. However, in legendary times Sorapiss was a man, a peace-loving king forced by circumstances to transform himself into this mighty, rugged rock mass. His capricious daughter Misurina had been promised a magical mirror by a local witch in exchange for shade for her abode, and this was inevitably provided by indulgent daddy-cum-mountain. Appreciative at a considerably later date of his sacrifice, Misurina wept tears of regret to fill a lake, which continues to reflect the massive form of her petrified father.

Lake near Rif. Vandelli

Those attempting the traverse (of average difficulty) should do so only in the best of weather, as altitudes over 2300m are reached, numerous short tracts with a little exposure are involved, and in early summer the chances are good of late-lying snow patches concealing waymarking. However its beauty lies in the peace and quiet and preponderance of animals over two-footed visitors, combined with breathtaking views.

Access to start point:
Passo Tre Croci road pass can be reached by car from Cortina on the panoramic SS 48 which continues to Auronzo, after a turn-off for Misurina.

Dolomiti Bus ensures several daily links July to mid-Sept between Cortina and Misurina.

STAGE ONE: TO RIF. VANDELLI (2HR)

Not far east of the hotel at **Passo Tre Croci** (1805m) is the start of a former First World War military mule track, signed n.215. Going southeast initially, it heads into the wood and offers essentially level walking at the base of the Marcoira and Loudo mountains for over an hour, passing a couple of overgrown forts. Ahead southeast is the rugged Marmarole range, and you often glimpse the waterfall mentioned above. On the edge of a steep-sided valley the path turns up for the first of a series of **metal ladders**, straightforward passages without notable exposure. As the path resumes its southern direction, the wood opens up and there's a longish narrow stretch aided by a guiding cable.

With the gain in altitude, the tree cover is springy dwarf mountain pine for the most part, interspersed with larch. Keep your eyes on the ground as a fascinating fossil

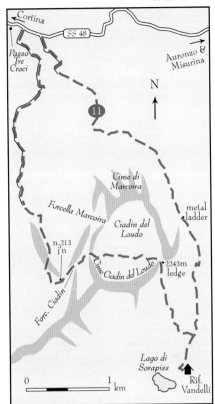

zone is encountered: underfoot is dark soil mixed with white rock embedded with surprising numbers of heart-shaped outlines of Megalodonts, bivalve shells averaging 10cm in length from the upper Triassic, 215–223 million years ago.

Not far up is modest **Rif. Vandelli** (1928m), which occupies a wonderful position, looking out north to the Cadini, the Sesto Dolomites and, of course, Misurina's lake in the distance. The nearby Lago di Sorapiss is quite delightful; its unusually translucent green-blue waters owe their milky appearance to suspended powdered debris from the three shrinking frontal glaciers on the awe-inspiring north-facing wall of Punta Sorapiss, the grandiose backdrop. Directly above the lake is the rocky point curiously referred to as Dito di Dio (Finger of God).

STAGE TWO: VIA FORCELLA CIADIN (1HR 30MIN) AND DESCENT TO PASSO TRE CROCI (1HR)

Backtrack on path n.215 downhill for about 10min from Rif. Vandelli, and branch left (northwest) on n.216, heading decidedly uphill in zigzags towards the Cime Ciadin del Loudo. Amongst the thinning trees and dwarf pines the chances of spotting the large herds of chamois increase as you climb. Their pale fawn coats are distinguishable on the scree and stand out against the green scrubby vegetation.

After an hour of steady ascent with astounding views onto the Tre Cime and neighbouring Cadini you arrive at an aided stretch via a short **ledge** (2243m). As it finishes and you enter the basin of the Ciadin del Loudo, take the unnumbered path (n.223 on the map) that forks off left (while straight ahead leads to Forcella Marcoira, an alternative if rather steep descent route). It cuts across a scree slope heading essentially west, and where the path becomes faint or disappears the way is marked by the occasional orange triangle and 3 (for the Alta Via 3) and heaps of stones. Half an hour on is **Forcella Ciadin** (2378m), another brief aided rock passage, rating average on exposure.

The view here is dominated by the elegant spires and points of the wonderful Cristallo group (north). A short way around is a signed junction for n.213 where you need to abandon the high-level traverse and start the drop (north). Mixed wood is traversed and the final stretch is on a forestry track for the straightforward return to **Passo Tre Croci** (1805m).

Tourist Office Cortina d'Ampezzo
tel. 0436-3231/3232

Rif. A. Vandelli
tel. 0435-39015 CAI,
sleeps 57,
open 20/6–20/9

12 – Antelao-Marmarole: Val d'Oten

Walking time	5hr + 40min for cascades (less 2hr if drive to Capanna degli Alpini)
Walk distance	17.5km/10.8 miles
Difficulty	Grade 1–2
Ascent/descent	975m/975m (less 350m if drive to Capanna degli Alpini)
Map	Tabacco n.016 scale 1:25,000
Start point	Praciadelan, Val d'Oten

The wild Antelao-Marmarole range is a massive barrier separating the well-visited Valle d'Ampezzo and the quieter Calalzo valley to the east. A convoluted series of rock spires and soaring points, it is brought to a fitting conclusion in the south by the unsurpassed 3264m of the Antelao, 'king of the Dolomites', whose unmistakable pyramidal shape is recognisable from a great distance. A chamois hunter Matteo Ossi is believed to be the first to have scaled it, however the budding Viennese climber Paul Grohmann accompanied by guides from Cortina officially claimed the honour in 1863.

The range as a whole is infamous for the fearful avalanches and rockslides it has sent hurtling downhill over the centuries, many a village irretrievably engulfed by deadly rivers of stone. Rumour has it these catastrophes were the work of the spiteful Croderes, who occupied ice palaces amongst the dizzy snowbound peaks.

The first stage of the walk follows pretty Val d'Oten, lovely for picnics, through which runs a torrent that continually changes course through a deep scree bed. The valley owes its shape to ancient glacial shaping, though the characteristic U has since been altered by the large amount of splintered rock spilling down its flanks.

According to an endearing story, this mountain is really the petrified body of the giant Antelao, whose only misdeed was to fall in love, against the will of a wicked witch. Her powerful curse turned him into stone and he pitched headlong into the Val d'Oten, his heart an unpretentious glacier the icy-blue colour of forget-me-not flowers.

Val d'Oten

Access to start point:
From Calalzo on the SS 51bis, the Val d'Oten breaks off northwest for the surfaced 11.5km stretch to Praciadelan and Bar alla Pineta, where you can park. The remaining 4.3km from Praciadelan to Capanna degli Alpini is open to private traffic, but the going can be rough as it is unfailingly washed away in spring. Public transport (Dolomiti Bus or train) takes you only as far as Calalzo.

Its thick forests in the middle-range altitudes shelter bountiful roe deer, whereas the open meadows are a paradise for marmots and resplendent wild flowers, which flourish right up to the base of the ice field on the Antelao. There has been serious discussion about the establishment of a park encompassing the Marmarole, Antelao and the Sorapiss groups to protect such natural wealth as well as keeping tighter checks on hunting, though unfortunately nothing concrete has come of it to date.

With regard to practical matters, a number of bars and restaurants can be found along Val d'Oten, but the only shops are back down at Calalzo. Stage One along a dirt track is elementary and for everyone, while the climb to the hut in Stage Two is straightforward, if steep at times, and makes use of a good path.

STAGE ONE: PRACIADELAN TO CAPANNA DEGLI ALPINI (1HR)

From **Praciadelan** (1044m) the bumpy gravel track marked as n.255 proceeds westward, penetrating deep into the Marmarole in almost imperceptible ascent. Thick wood alternates with fan-shaped cones of detritus, the bleached white rock quite dazzling at times. The watercourse, Torrente Oten, is accessible at many points and affords good views over to M. Ciaudierona, the elongated crest south. After an impressive scree flow beneath the Cresta Vanedel, you reach **Capanna degli Alpini** (1395m), a bright, hospitable hut nestling on the edge of cool conifer forest.•

STAGE TWO: ASCENT TO RIF. GALASSI (1HR 45MIN)

From **Capanna degli Alpini** ample signed path n.255 starts its leisurely ascent west through woods, where a wealth of wild orchids bloom in early summer. Dominated by conifers, this is the perfect habitat for the spectacular capercaillie grouse, a rare sight for the lucky few, particularly in autumn when out scouting for laden bilberry shrubs. In easy curves the path ascends to a pasture clearing before following the stream bed for a fair stretch. Once you've decidedly crossed over, there are tight zigzags up rather stark terrain anchored by dwarf mountain pines, with views to the Antelao and its tongue of ice from pocket glaciers increasing in impressiveness.

The simple stone building **Rif. Galassi** (2018m), formerly military premises, occupies a spectacular position, literally around the corner from one of the remnant

•**Side trip to Cascata delle Pile (40min return)**
A signed path for the lovely waterfall climbs stiffly in a very short distance, hugging the edge of a gorge. Remember that it will feel even steeper on the way back and watch your step in wet conditions.

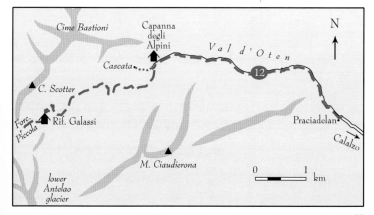

Tourist Office Calalzo
tel. 0435-32348

Capanna degli Alpini,
private, sleeps 10, open
July–Sept

Rif. Galassi
tel. 0436-9685 CAI,
sleeps 110, open
mid-June to mid-Sept

glaciers on the Antelao and facing soaring Cima Scotter (north). Nearby 2120m **Forcella Piccola** is a must for the views along the western flank of the Marmarole, not to mention over Valle d'Ampezzo. The pass is a fault line that divides the Dolomite rock that constitutes the Marmarole to the north from the limestone that makes up the Antelao massif to the south. The latter is particularly vulnerable to the dissolving effect of rainwater, and fascinating examples of karstification are visible a matter of minutes along path n.250, another worthwhile side trip.

STAGE THREE: DESCENT VIA CAPANNA DEGLI ALPINI (1HR 15MIN) AND RETURN TO PRACIADELAN (1HR)

The return route to the valley floor follows the same paths as the ascent via **Capanna degli Alpini** (1395m) then on to the parking area at **Praciadelan** (1044m).

Remnant of the Antelao's lower glacier near Rif. Galassi

13 – Spalti di Toro-Monfalconi: Rif. Padova to Rif. Tita Barba

Walking time	4hr
Walk distance	11.5km/7.2 miles
Difficulty	Grade 2
Ascent/descent	700m/700m
Maps	Tabacco n.016 scale 1:25,000
Start point	parking area near Rif. Padova

Apart from a steepish climb in the middle section, this route amounts to an averagely difficult walk, well worth it in early summer for the abundance of unusual wild flowers such as the lady's slipper orchid, not to mention golden colours in autumn. The hospitable refuges encountered can provide both meals and accommodation. An extension loop via Forcella Spè is feasible for those with some experience, a nose for directions and a good map – see the description following Stage Three.

A glorious foray into the beautiful peaceful reaches of the Spalti di Toro-Monfalconi, one of the many wild Dolomite ranges found in the far eastern sector of the Cadore, on the border with Carnia, and well off the mainstream tourist track. Thick and often impenetrable conifer forest clothes the valleys right up to the reign of rock and scree, providing shelter for elusive deer and squirrels, though the many clearings for summer farms and wood choppers afford sweeping views of the group's magnificent spires and towers.

Monfalconi-Spalti di Toro from Casera Vedorcia

Access to start point:
From Domegge di Cadore, Via S. Giorgio turns south off the main road SS 51bis next to an old timber enoteca wine cellar. It traverses a square with a church and renowned pastry shop before heading down across Lago di Centro Cadore. The ensuing 8.5km, still surfaced but much narrower and with a couple of hairy bends, climb the cleft valley with Torrente Talagona to the parking area just before Rif. Padova.

While Domegge is served by the year-round Dolomiti Bus, the road (or alternative path) to Rif. Padova means 3hr on foot, so without a car the walk is only feasible with an overnight stay at the hut.

Stage One: parking area via Rif. Padova to Torrente Talagona (1hr)

A matter of minutes from the parking area is the culinary haven that is the picturesque and homely **Rif. Padova** (1287m), set on the lower edge of 'Thor's meadows' (Pra' di Toro) and complete with a summer dairy farm (Casera), facing the magnificent spread of the Spalti di Toro-Monfalconi rock spires. The original 1909 refuge with alpine garden occupied a higher position, but was swept away by an avalanche in 1932.

Path n.350, signed for Casera Vedorcia, makes its way through thick conifer forest, climbing and winding around Collalto. Next you're in for a lengthy descent along a series of watercourses, and eventually come to the **bridge over Torrente Talagona** and a signed junction (with a link to the road from Domegge). It's worth halting here to explore the inviting pools and cascades.

Stage Two: to Casera Vedorcia (1hr) then Rif. Tita Barba (20min)

A short distance uphill close to a hut at 1360m, a branch path turns off due south (extension loop – see below), whereas this route proceeds west, climbing particularly steeply on this stretch. Luckily numerous gaps in the trees provide mountain views and an excuse for a rest.

On emerging from the forest, you cross pasture slopes and will need to climb right off the path through thick nettles to reach the summer dairy farm **Casera Vedorcia** (1704m) and its marvellous panoramic setting. Between M. Cridola (east-northeast) and the Spalti di Toro-Monfalconi line-up is Forcella Scodavacca, the name a curious reference to a pioneering shepherd from the 1300s sent to colonise these pastures. Threatened by invaders, he set off a massive rockslide which unfortunately struck a number of his cows or *vacca* in Italian, buried but for their tail – *coda*! The isolated tower Campanile di Val Montanaia can be seen to the southeast, a well-known testing ground for rock climbers.

In the 1860s the celebrated English writers and

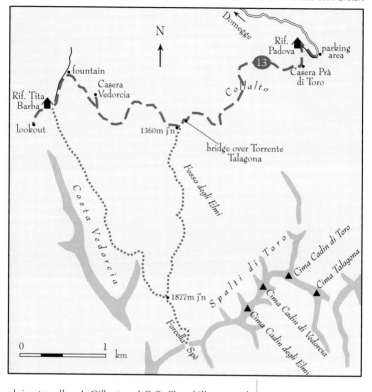

alpine travellers J. Gilbert and G.C. Churchill ventured this far, attracted by the Spalti–Monfalconi group, and counted a total of 30 rocky points and spires.

Go back below the buildings to resume the path which ducks in and out between a series of timber chalets to reach a fountain and jeep track (signed fork). This leads south-ish up to **Rif. Tita Barba** (1821m), an idyllic Hansel and Gretel house in a picturesque flowered clearing, which offers basic amenities but hearty local dishes.

On the far side a clear path leads (5min) over to a marvellous lookout towards the Marmarole, Antelao and Pelmo.

Rif. Tita Barba

STAGE THREE: RETURN TO RIF. PADOVA (1HR 40MIN)

Go back to Rif. Padova and the parking area the same way.

Tourist Office Calalzo
tel. 0435-32348

Rif. Padova
tel. 0435-72488 CAI,
sleeps 50,
open 1/5–1/11

Rif. Tita Barba
tel. 0435-32902
private, sleeps 16,
open 15/6–25/9

Extension to Forcella Spè

Soon after Torrente Talagona in Stage Two, path n.352 breaks off due south via Fosso degli Elmi for Forcella Spè (2049m). The way is not always clear or as scenic as the main route described. A short distance before the actual *forcella*, wider path n.350 is encountered (1877m junction), and from here a panoramic stretch leads north-northwest to Rif. Tita Barba, then you follow the main route for the return to Rif. Padova. An extra 1hr 30min–2hr should be calculated.

14 – The Pramper Circuit

Walking time	4hr 15min (6hr 30min from Forno di Zoldo)
Walk distance	14.5km/9 miles
Difficulty	Grade 1–2
Ascent/descent	800m/800m (1050m/1050m from Forno di Zoldo)
Map	Tabacco n.025 scale 1:25,000
Start point	Pian de la Fopa, Val Pramper

Branching south off the Val di Zoldo, a mere crow's flight from the landmark Pelmo and Civetta, is quiet Val Pramper in the realms of the Dolomiti Bellunesi National Park. Bounded by minor but memorable mountains and clad in thick conifer woods with the occasional clearing used for pastoral purposes, it is well worth exploring.

The Val Pramper receives far fewer visitors than its more famous neighbours – though the long-distance Alta Via 1 transits in the upper part – and consequently abounds in animal life in the shape of chamois and marmots, as well as wonderful wild flowers and even First World War relics. Both ample tracks and clearly marked paths are followed on this straightforward loop itinerary, and you stay below the tree line, with a maximum altitude of 1940m above sea level. A family-run hut, Rif. Pramperet, is visited, and while its water is deemed unsuitable for drinking, the simple home-style food can be sampled without apprehension.

STAGE ONE: PIAN DE LA FOPA TO RIF. PRAMPERET (2HR)

From the car park at **Pian de la Fopa** (1210m) the rough road (or n.523) continues southwest parallel to the watercourse surrounded by conifer wood. On the opposite bank of the stream rises the Spiz di Mezzodì massif with its countless spires and peaks, whose erosion results in remarkable rivers of scree – check your map for Giaron de la Fopa, reputedly one of the most extensive in the whole of the Dolomites. As the track starts to climb westward facing the rambling San Sebastiano group, an old

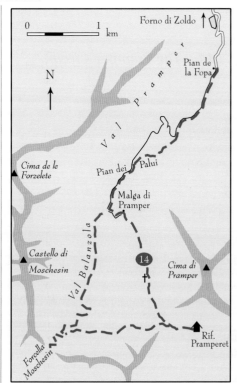

Access to start point:
Val di Zoldo is accessible via the SS 251 between Longarone and Caprile, with links to the Boite and Cordevole valleys, and Forno di Zoldo is the main township. It is served by Dolomiti Bus 12 months a year from Belluno via Longarone railway station.

To reach the start point by car, from the western extremity of Forno di Zoldo near the church of Sant'Antonio (868m) take the narrow road south over the stream (Torrente Mae) and keep left, following signs for Rif. Sommariva al Pramperet. Alternating surfaced and rough sections, it climbs steeply through forest and into Val Pramper, levelling out. Shortly after a dam the road is barred to unauthorised vehicles and there's a small car park at Pian de la Fopa.

On foot, allow about 1hr 15min for this 5km stretch uphill.

path cuts the corner, rejoining on a pasture clearing. The presence of numerous streams here and consequent marshy terrain has encouraged a wealth of dainty aquatic plants and interesting grass species, and has given the flat its apt name Pian dei Palui (Plain of the marshes).

Not far up is route n.540 (the return route), but you stick to the track as far as the nearby dairy farm **Malga di Pramper** (1hr, 1540m), set in an ancient glacial basin. From here path n.523 proceeds sout-southeast, ascending steeply at times through larch and across a relatively recent landslide, curving beneath the foot of imposing Cima di Pramper. After a shrine on a rise at 1753m is the lush pasture zone of Pra de la Vedova (the Widow's meadow), which owes its fertility to an underlying strata of clay which holds in moisture. In 1995 a Mesolithic camp site (10,000–6500 years old) was discovered here, once used by seasonal hunters tracking a variety of deer, ibex and chamois. It is strewn with chunks of rock which have detached themselves from neighbouring mountains.

Rif. Pramperet (1857m) is a simple wooden establishment beautifully located on the edge of a vast meadow overlooking a deep valley in front of the wild Cime de Zita and Talvena, while to the west-northwest is the triangle of M. Tamer.

STAGE TWO: TRAVERSE VIA FORCELLA MOSCHESIN (45MIN) AND DESCENT TO PIAN DE LA FOPA (1HR 30MIN)

After a stretch in common with the arrival route, you strike out in a westerly direction on n.543 (also marked with the triangle for Alta Via 1) through unusual thickets of springy dwarf mountain pines, the perfect habitat for clumsy black grouse. The occasional opening dotted with larch will reveal extraordinary numbers of martagon lilies for early summer walkers, as well as some stunning views of the Pelmo massif, due north, rising unmistakably above the sea of dark green conifers. You merge with the old military path n.540 to climb the final 100m to **Forcella Moschesin** (1940m), an ample saddle bright with alpenrose shrubs and blue bellflowers. The rock surfaces all around conceal shelters and tunnel systems dating back to the First World War, while close by stands a sizeable ruined barracks (*ex caserma*) in pale stone from 1913. Keep your eyes peeled here for abrupt movements on the impervious rock faces for the chamois mountain goats which give themselves away by dislodging loose stones.

For the ensuing descent backtrack to where n.540 forks off to descend north down Val Balanzola in wide curves under the so-called Castello di Moschesin, an offshoot of the Tamer group. It rejoins the ascent track a stone's throw from **Malga di Pramper** (1540m), and from there on you need the rough road once more to return to **Pian de la Fopa** (1210m).

Tourist Office Forno di Zoldo
tel. 0437-787349

Rif. Pramperet
tel. 0337-528403 CAI,
sleeps 40,
open 20/6–20/9

15 – The Pelmo and the Dinosaur Footprints

Walking time	4hr 30min
Walk distance	15km/9.4 miles
Difficulty	Grade 1–2
Ascent/descent	600m/600m
Map	Tabacco n.025 scale 1:25,000
Start point	Passo Staulanza

Dinosaurs, tropical tidal flats and a stocky 3168m Dolomite massif would not appear to have much in common. However some 220 million years ago, three distinct small-scale specimens ambled through shallows off a tropical beach and left a spate of footprints. Tide levels dropped little by little, calcareous deposits followed on and were compressed into rock, while the tracks themselves were preserved in fossil form. The earth-moving events that shaped the Alps saw the beds uplifted thousands of metres above their original position, while the elements did the rest in modelling. Ongoing erosion was responsible for a fortuitous rockfall in the not too distant past when an oblique slab was revealed, patterned with over 100 separate prints, identified as dinosaur prints (plaster casts are kept at the museum at Selva di Cadore).

The Pelmo is one of the easiest Dolomites to identify due to its majestic isolated shape and delicate ledges which catch the snow so effectively. It is better appreciated from a distance, as described by Gilbert and Churchill in 1864: 'For an hour the Pelmo … rose clear above the near green slopes of the valley northward … all but the very battlements free from cloud; a pale salmon-tinted, glistening mass, shooting upward from its hidden base below into the eddying mists above; a spectacle not of the earth but of the sky, in its cerulean tints and aerial architecture.'

The walk skirts the entire southern flank of the mountain, rates as fairly easy and entails relatively little height gain and loss. The only tricky tract is the last leg of the steepish path leading to the fossilised dinosaur footprints, as the earth is clayey and slippery even in the absence of rain. On the other hand the main path has lengthy muddy and marshy stretches, and longer walking times should be allowed after heavy rain as numerous detours become necessary and waterproof footwear comes into its own.

Val di Zoldo, whose quiet villages live in the shadow of two giants – the Pelmo and Civetta, comes alive in the winter months as a popular ski centre. In late medieval times, as place names such as Forno (furnace) and Fusine (forge) testify, it was important for iron-making and exported quality nails that were in great demand for shoes and shipbuilding, especially in Venice.

The magnificent Pelmo, seen from the southwest

A pleasant family-run refuge-guesthouse, Rif. Passo Staulanza, is located at the pass where the walk starts, while historic Rif. Venezia serves as the destination. The latter, erected in 1892, was the very first Italian refuge in the Dolomites and belongs to the Venice branch of the Italian Alpine Club (CAI).

The walk returns along the same route and can be varied by taking the alternative descent to Mareson, instead of returning to the pass – total timing is unchanged.

STAGE ONE: PASSO STAULANZA TO ORME TURN-OFF (45MIN)

From **Passo Staulanza** (1766m) you need path n.472, clearly marked for the 'Orme di Dinosauro' (dinosaur footprints). It climbs gently southeast through shady conifer wood inhabited by roe deer, and you keep right at the junction encountered after a matter of minutes. Dips and rises succeed one another, and gaps in the foliage allow glimpses of the snow-tipped Marmolada and the magnificent Civetta across the valley. The going is easy, and 45min along is the signed **Orme turn-off** (left) at 1890m for the climb to the dinosaur footprints.

STAGE TWO: DINOSAUR FOOTPRINTS (30MIN RETURN)

The prominent toppled slab bearing the prints and marked by a pole is visible uphill throughout your ascent.

Access to start point:
The SS 251 for the Val di Zoldo branches northwest off the main Piave valley at Longarone, and drops via Val Fiorentina and Selva di Cadore to Caprile on the SS 203.

Val di Zoldo is served by Dolomiti Bus all year long, while the extension to Passo Staulanza, the start point, only runs from beginning of July to mid-Sept.

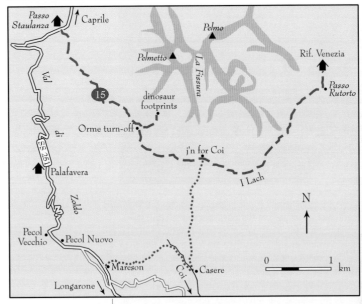

You follow a watercourse at first through thinning dwarf mountain pine and clamber up a red earth flank, where the clay underfoot is quite slippery when wet. Off to the right is a curious section of red-green-grey tinted geological beds uncovered by flowing water. Marmots are everywhere. The position is simply incredible, and the slab in question clearly broke off the Pelmetto, which accounts for the southwest corner of the giant Pelmo. The **dinosaur footprints** (2050m) themselves are quite impressive, if not that large. Views take in the Sella group to the northwest in addition to the glacier-bound Marmolada.

Return to the **Orme turn-off** on the main path the same way (15min), with due care on the initial slippery tract.

STAGE THREE: TO RIF. VENEZIA (1HR 15MIN)

Turn left onto n.472, and two links to Palafavera are shortly passed. Due east now, marshy and muddy tracts are traversed with the help of boards and bridges. The area is known Le Mandre (flocks), erstwhile pasture, while the route itself was the Triol dei Cavai (horses' track) and is mostly level. A veritable sea of dwarf mountain pine and juniper sees you rounding the dramatic and gradually changing mass of the Pelmo. A little over 15min from the Orme turn-off is the junction for n.473 and Coi, used by the alternative descent described below. Uphill at this point is the awe-inspiring profound cleft (La Fissura) which divides the Pelmo proper from the Pelmetto.

A slight rise through flowered meadows brings views northeast to the Marmarole. Now you drop beneath the Pelmo's southeast shoulder, awesome soaring cliffs. This basin is known as I Lach, a reference to water, and was the site of seasonal settlements in prehistoric times. A final short climb leads out to Passo Rutorto (1931m) for a superb view of the full line-up of the Marmarole, crowned by the Sorapiss. **Rif. Venezia** (1948m) is just around the corner.

STAGE FOUR: RETURN TO PASSO STAULANZA (2HR)

As per the outward route, take the same path for the scenic route back to Passo Staulanza.

Rock slab and fossilised dinosaur footprints below the Pelmo

Rif. Venezia looks over to the Sorapiss

Tourist Office Zoldo Alto (Mareson) tel. 0437-789145

Rif. Monte Pelmo (Palafavera) tel. 0437-789359, private, sleeps 8, open mid-June–end Sept

Rif. Palafavera tel. 0437-789133, private, sleeps 24, open mid-June to mid-Sept

Rif. Passo Staulanza tel. 0437-788566, private, sleeps 30, open 10/6–30/9

Rif. Venezia tel. 0436-9684 CAI, sleeps 75, open 20/6–20/9

Alternative descent to Mareson (1hr)

From the **junction for Coi** mentioned above in Stage Three, n.473 drops quickly, widening into a farm track. Half an hour down at **Casere** (1618m), a strategic fork with a hut and precious drinking fountain, turn right along the level track. Minutes along is n.498, a lovely shady old path branching off left. A little way down ignore the turn-off left (marked 'Colonia' on a rock) and keep straight on for the nearby pond (*laghetto*). Here the path heads diagonally down for the final 10min to the hamlet of **Mareson** (1334m), with main road, bus stop and tourist office.

16 – Around the Croda da Lago

Walking time	4hr 45min (6hr 30min on foot from Pocol)
Walk distance	12.5km/7.7 miles
Difficulty	Grade 2
Ascent/descent	760m/760m (960m/960m on foot from Pocol)
Map	Tabacco n.03 scale 1:25,000
Start point	Ponte di Rocurto

Croda da Lago is a relatively modest Dolomite formation a short distance southwest of Cortina, but memorable for its elegant slender profile and ridge of jagged points – to the joy of rock climbers. This lovely walk makes a complete circle of the mountain and also takes in the unusual neighbouring Laston di Formin, a gigantic inclined table-like slab that rears up alongside Croda da Lago. Its constituent rock is a type of Dolomite from the so-called Dürrenstein formation, which reaches a thickness of 450m here, a record for these mountains.

A final note of interest concerns the high-altitude pasture zone encountered in Stage Two. Around 10,000 years ago it was used on a seasonal basis by Mesolithic hunters of ibex and deer. They would take refuge under a prominent overhanging boulder a short way downhill (one of 24 sites) and left an enormous quantity of implements in bone, flint and rock crystal, not to mention the skeleton of a 40-year-old Cro-Magnon male in a ritualised burial. The intriguing finds are on display at the museum of Selva di Cadore in Val Fiorentina (c/o Comune tel. 0437-720100).

The height gain and loss during the walk make it a fair hike, but all effort is amply compensated by wonderful views. Overall it rates average on difficulty,

Numerous legends originated in the Croda da Lago area featuring marmot princesses, eagles, lost treasures and enchanted maidens who dwelt in mountain streams. Perhaps the most curious concerns the origin of the larch tree. The sole conifer that is not evergreen and loses its needles with the onset of winter, it was purportedly invented by the forest animals and dwarves as a wedding gift for their generous benefactor and queen. The original version was a delicate plant put together with fronds and bunches of wild flowers that quickly withered. However, the queen covered it with her filmy veil, and this is reproduced each spring as the fresh green lacy vegetation shoots.

Crossing Rio Costeana on the way to Rif. Palmieri

Access to start point:
From Pocol on the outskirts of Cortina, take the SS 638 towards Passo Giau. About 4.5km up is the start point, and roadside parking is possible. The closest public transport reaches Pocol (local Cortina bus or the July to mid-Sept Dolomiti Bus to Passo Falzarego), and you can either try your hand at hitchhiking on the Passo Giau road or set out on the path described below.

•Access from Pocol (1hr)
About 1.5km (15min) up the road from Pocol towards Passo Giau, n.434 is signposted. Heading due south, it climbs steadily through the wood to join the main route at **Cason di Formin** (1885m).

though Stage One can be attempted on its own by beginners or those on their first holiday outing – it entails an easy, gentle ascent of a mere 300m as far as the lovely alpine hut Rif. Palmieri, set on the shore of a pretty lake. Stage Three on the other hand sees very few walkers, and traverses fascinating wild, rock-ridden terrain, all but devoid of vegetation.

STAGE ONE: VIA CASON DI FORMIN (30MIN) TO RIF. PALMIERI (1HR)

A little downstream from the bridge known as **Ponte di Rocurto** (1700m), a signpost points you east onto path n.437. A dip into the lovely shady wood and you traverse the Rio Costeana watercourse via a photogenic log bridge, just one of many such crossings. One especially noteworthy stream with cascades precedes a log cabin and junction with the path from Pocol, at **Cason di Formin** (1885m). •

As n.434, the path passes the turn-off for Val Formin and the return route. A steepish section follows, after which reward comes in the shape of a marvellous **lookout point**. The breadth of the views of quite astonishing after all that wood: to the west-northwest are the isolated Cinque Torri; to the west-southwest the point of the Nuvolau and its hut; to the northwest are the Tofane; while north-northeast over Cortina is the Pomagagnon; and due east lies the magnificent Sorapiss.

From here on you follow the Val Negra, and there is

easy, mostly level walking to pretty Lago Federa and then charming **Rif. Palmieri** (2046m), beneath the graceful eastern wall of the Croda da Lago. The hut took its name from a Second World War partisan from Bologna, and offers a jeep taxi link with Zuel, south of Cortina.

STAGE TWO: VIA FORCELLA AMBRIZZOLA (45MIN) THEN FORCELLA ROSSA DI FORMIN (45MIN)

A marvellous straightforward route (n.434) leads southwards below soaring rock points to **Forcella Ambrizzola** (2227m), a key passage between the Croda da Lago and the Becco di Mezzodì, southwest. A broad swathe of fertile high-altitude pasture used by the odd sheep slopes southward, and it is here that the Mesolithic finds mentioned in the preface were unearthed. The majestic Pelmo is visible now, along with many other groups, though the views will naturally improve from the next pass.

Turn right (northwest) on n.436 towards Passo Giau, then fork off right after 10min for the steady climb up scree to the breathtaking **Forcella Rossa di Formin** (2462m), also known as Forcella dei Lastoni di Formin, right under Cima Ambrizzola. The magnificent panorama is dominated by the Tofane, due north. The Lastoni di Formin, or 'great slabs,' extend westward in this bizarre landscape, rent with

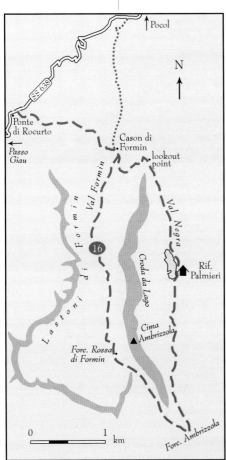

The Croda da Lago and Rif. Palmieri from Forcella Ambrizzola

Tourist Office Cortina d'Ampezzo tel. 0436-3231/3232

Rif. Palmieri tel. 0436-862085 CAI, sleeps 35, open 15/6–30/9 then Oct weekends.

gigantic cracks than run deep into the rock. Time and weather permitting, follow the cairns off the main route westward, watching your step.

STAGE THREE: DESCENT TO CASON DI FORMIN (1HR 15MIN) THEN RETURN TO PONTE DI RUCORTO (30MIN)

You follow the west wall of the Croda da Lago quite closely for most of the ensuing descent amidst fallen boulders and scree. The lower part brings you to Val Formin and the welcome return to greenery then **Cason di Formin** (1885m). Turn left onto n.437 for the final stretch back to the road at **Ponte di Rocurto** (1700m).

17 – Up the Nuvolau

Walking time	4hr 15min
Walk distance	13km/8.1 miles
Difficulty	Grade 1–2
Ascent/descent	700m/700m
Map	Tabacco n.03 scale 1:25,000
Start point	Passo Falzarego

Though nothing near as impressive as the majestic groups opposite, the Averau–Nuvolau–Cinque Torri complex is easy to reach and justifiably well trodden. It offers some varied worthwhile walking, particularly suitable for beginners, while the Cinque Torri (Five Towers), a clutter of jagged teeth set in grassy gums, exert a special magnetism for acrobatic climbers.

The route, average in terms of difficulty, is clear and easy to follow, and can be shortened by using the chair lift and bus on the final leg. During the first stage several rock gullies are encountered, one including a brief elementary clamber, but nothing exposed. En route are a number of refuges which can provide shelter and refreshments/meals.

STAGE ONE: PASSO FALZAREGO VIA FORCELLA AVERAU (1HR 10MIN) TO RIF. AVERAU (20MIN)

When you've had your fill of the tantalising alpine kitsch (flanked by a good selection of maps) at Passo Falzarego (2108m), locate the start of path n.441 behind the blue-shuttered bar/shop. It climbs gently southeast across grassy hillsides towards the Averau mountain massif. A popular skiing area in winter, in summer red clay is usually exposed and the slopes can be muddy. Higher up the terrain becomes rockier and calcareous, as testified by the yellow Rhaetian poppies and pink thrift-like

The ample road pass Passo Falzarego that links the Cortina valley with Val Badia is an excellent mountain viewing point: begin with the Lagazuoi Piccolo directly above with its cable-car to the north, the awesome Tofane threesome to the northeast, and move back to Sorapiss and the Antelao to the east beyond Cortina. Far away (southwest) is the Marmolada and its glacier preceded by rounded Col di Lana, while closer at hand (southeast) is a group of low-set heterogeneous mountains, vast inclined slabs rising up from pasture slopes.

Access to start point:
Passo Falzarego is served by summer buses from Cortina and Belluno (Dolomiti Bus, July to mid-Sept) as well as Corvara/Kurvar in Val Badia/Gadertal (SAD, late June to mid-Sept). Otherwise for private vehicles it can be reached from three directions: the SS 48 from Cortina, the continuation of which also transits in tight curves via Cernadoi, and the SS 203 from Alleghe, while drivers from the Val Badia will need the turn-off at La Villa/Stern.

Rif. Nuvolau's view to the Lastoni di Formin and the Croda da Lago

blooms, whereas occasional grass patches are brightened by gentians which last well into autumn. The climb steepens as you enter the first of a series of gullies, with Lago de Limedes visible downhill. Waymarking is regular, with red and white painted stripes on rocks. At a level area with *cima* (summit) painted on a rock (pointing right for Punta Gallina), turn sharp left instead to climb steeply up a final rough but brief gully, where you clamber round a huge boulder. Continuing on a level path you are soon joined by a path from Rif. Col Gallina.

Straight ahead is **Forcella Averau** (2435m), stronghold of a flock of jet black alpine choughs. Having taken in the vast panorama southwards, turn left (southeast) on the lower path. It is mostly level walking cutting across scree, skirting the crumbling southern wall of the Averau, to Forcella Nuvolau and privately run **Rif. Averau** (2416m). This cheery refuge is lined with excellent photos of local animal life, and boasts a great terrace looking south taking in the Marmolada to the Pale di San Martino, Civetta and the wild Monti del Sole, amongst others.

STAGE TWO: ASCENT TO RIF. NUVOLAU AND RETURN (1HR TOTAL)

From Rif. Averau go east to the nearby junction for the long ridge right (southeast) up the Nuvolau. Straightforward and popular path n.439 follows this

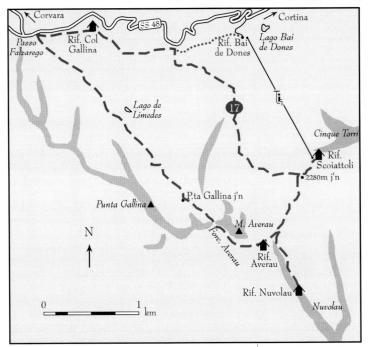

unusual broad rock incline for 150m to **Rif. Nuvolau** (2575m), perched on the summit. The original building dated back to the late 1800s and was the property of the Alpine Club of Cortina, and could be reached on horseback via a special bridle track. Alas, Austrian artillery put paid to the building during the 1915–18 conflict, so the present hut is relatively new – 1930. The atmosphere here is unique, and on those days when the mountain does 'betray' its name (*nuvola* means cloud), the views range from the graceful shape of nearby Averau, the Tofane massif and the Cristallo east over Cortina and even as far west as the snow-capped Ortles and the Austrian Alps.

The descent to the turn-off above Rif. Averau follows the same route as the ascent.

STAGE THREE: TO RIF. SCOIATTOLI (15MIN) THEN PASSO FALZAREGO (1HR 30MIN)

From the junction near Rif. Averau, head right (north-northeast) along the wide path alongside the bulldozered ski slopes towards the odd Cinque Torri rock formations and **Rif. Scoiattoli** (2225m). The name of this welcoming family-run refuge refers to the famous Cortina-based rock climbing team, the Squirrels.

Leave some time to explore the squarish blocks of the Cinque Torri – the lowest one is the Torre Inglese, the English tower – and admire the climbers. Alongside the towers is a maze of trenches and shelters dating back to the First World War, and recently restored for visitors.

An **alternative exit** route at this point is via the nearby chair lift which will drop you down at Rif. Bai de Dones 1889m (no accommodation), close to the road (bus stop) 3.5km below Passo Falzarego.

Just back from Rif. Scoiattoli is a **2280m junction** on a crest where n.440 branches off (west at first) to traverse a rocky mountainside. The narrowing path crosses sparse wood with mixed conifers and dwarf pines on the final stretch, amidst a colourful array of wild flowers. An hour should suffice down to the marshy meadows and the road 2.5km below the pass. Stick to the left-hand side of the road on the unmarked path which cuts the road bends. A further half an hour via hospitable **Rif. Col Gallina** (2054m) and you're back at **Passo Falzarego** again.

Tourist Office Cortina
d'Ampezzo
tel. 0436-3231/3232

Rif. Averau
tel. 0436-4660 private,
sleeps 21, open 1/6–30/9

Rif. Col Gallina
tel. 0436-2939 private,
sleeps 15,
open mid-June–late Sept

Rif. Nuvolau
tel. 0436-867938 CAI,
sleeps 26,
open 10/6–24/9

Rif. Scoiattoli
tel. 0436-867939
private, sleeps 20,
open 4/7–20/9

18 – Lagazuoi Piccolo: First World War Tunnels

Walking time	3hr 30min (less 1hr 30min if the cable-car is used) + 1hr extra for the alternative
Walk distance	4km/2.5 miles
Difficulty	Grade 3 (Grade 1–2 if the tunnels are excluded)
Ascent/descent	650m/650m (1100m in descent for the alternative)
Map	Tabacco n.03 scale 1:25,000
Start point	Passo Falzarego

Tragic events swept over these peaks with the outbreak of World War One. Passo Falzarego, one of the most strategically situated road passes in the Dolomites, close to the Austrian–Italian border, was a central arena for the conflict. All the surrounding mountains still bear extensive evidence of fortifications, artillery positions and strongholds, not to mention the massive damage effected by powerful mines. The face of Lagazuoi Piccolo, for example, was radically altered by explosions – the enormous cone-shaped mound of detritus directly under the cable-car line was the work of the Austrians, while a similar one further right comes courtesy of the Italians. Needless to say, the loss of life was devastating. Some ingenious engineering work was carried out with the excavation of some 11 tunnels through the mountainside – extraordinarily difficult given the precarious conditions and continual shelling. Furthermore, for example, M. Averau over the valley was fitted with spotlights to illuminate the face of Lagazuoi, where the two armies were busy in repeated attempts to dislodge each other.

At one point, with the purpose of taking the Austrian position on the Lagazuoi Piccolo summit, Italian forces

As the story goes, in times long past the soaring mountainous realms of the sprawling Fanis group in the Dolomites were home to the legendary Fanes people. Their greedy king, not satisfied with the kingdom's prosperity, arranged to betray his subjects in return for greater riches. However his pact with the enemy turned sour, his karma caught up with him and his petrified profile stands out to this day on Lagazuoi Piccolo, his long beard and crown of rocky points clearly visible from Passo Falzarego, aptly named for the *falso re*, or 'false king'!

SHORTER WALKS IN THE DOLOMITES

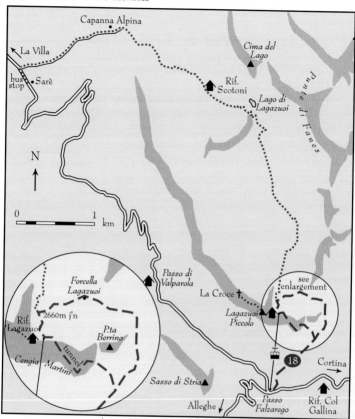

from their stronghold on the Cengia Martini ledge hewed out a 1100m-long tunnel climbing 230m and reaching 45° in parts. It has since been fitted with cables, ladders and steps to make visits possible, and is followed in Stage Two of this walk in descent, the more manageable direction. This exhilarating stretch is for experienced walkers only as it is steep and can be slippery, has several exposed tracts and entails a long stretch with no natural light. A torch is essential, and a head-lamp even better as it leaves your hands free. Old-style flare torches are on sale at Rif. Lagazuoi. Also suggested are boots with a non-slip sole and gloves to protect your hands while gripping the cable. If you prefer, you can entrust your rucksack to the cable-car for transport down to the pass for a modest fee.

At the time of writing, EU-funded summer work camps were underway around Piccolo Lagazuoi to restore more tunnels and fortified positions of the 1915–18 conflict and render them safe and accessible to the public, as a vast open-air museum. An illustrated guide is on sale, and the web site www.dolomiti.org/lagazuoi is also helpful.

If the tunnel route doesn't sound like your cup of tea, the alternative route to Sarè can be a rewarding (if fairly long) exit covering a total of 1100m in descent. You emerge on the road and can return to Passo Falzarego by way of the SAD bus.

Access to start point:
See Walk 17.

The Lagazuoi cable-car (which operates late May–early Nov) can be taken for the ascent, thereby cutting 1hr 20min off the walk time.

STAGE ONE: ASCENT FROM PASSO FALZAREGO VIA FORCELLA LAGAZUOI (1HR) TO RIF. LAGAZUOI (30MIN)

From **Passo Falzarego** (2108m), those who do not opt for the cable-car and embark on the 650m ascent should expect somewhat monotonous scree terrain with innumerable steep zigzags, compensated amply by wide-reaching views and a good chance of seeing chamois. Clear path n.402 strikes out in a northeast direction alongside winter ski slopes. Half an hour up it passes the fork left for the strategic ledge Cengia Martini and wartime tunnels (where the descent route rejoins in Stage Two) with plenty of rock windows visible. Tucked up under the soaring rock flanks of Punta Berrino on your left are remains of wartime huts and fortifications, while the slopes are scattered with old timber and even barbed wire.

Keep left at the fork for Forcella Lagazuoi to ascend a steep ski slope. The elongated rock barrier of Lagazuoi Grande, an extension south of the Fanis massif, is passed, and **Forcella Lagazuoi** (2573m) soon gained. This magnificent viewpoint overlooks the vast gentle stony slopes of the Alpe di Lagazuoi, backed by the stunning sheer rock flanks of the Punte di Fanes and Cima del Lago. Over south are the Averau, Nuvolau and their neighbours.

It's a short climb on n.401 to a **2660m junction** from where the Lago di Lagazuoi can be seen far below to the north. All that separates you now from the refuge and cable-car arrival station is a final steep climb, snow-covered until well into July. **Rif. Lagazuoi** (2752m) boasts a top-class restaurant and comfortable hotel-standard accommodation as well as dormitories, not to mention a marvellous panoramic terrace with name plates for identifying the multitude of mountains around.•

•Extension to La Croce (30min return)
From the terrace, a path proceeds west-northwest along the narrow ridge with a guiding hand-cable, to a further breathtaking lookout at a cross (2778m). Inadvisable for anyone who has trouble with heights.

STAGE TWO: DESCENT TO PASSO FALZAREGO VIA THE WWI MOUNTAINSIDE TUNNEL (1HR 30MIN)

Return to the cable-car station and follow the arrows for the *galleria* (Italian for tunnel), just below the concrete platform. The clear path with a cable hand-rail makes its way around left (east) past blown-up fortifications and via a crest where trench walkways have been reconstructed. The path enters a timbered doorway and 'disappears' into a hole (10min) for the start of the actual descent within the mountainside – a glance down inside the steep tunnel gives an idea of what's to come. A series of 'windows' provides dizzying views and the guiding cable is continuous, as is a series of steps, though the constant presence of water makes it slippery going, the difficulty compounded with a lack of natural light at times. En route are reconstructed storage depots, cramped sleeping quarters and eery side tunnels.

From La Croce lookout near Rif. Lagazuoi

About 1hr down will see you exit onto a broad ledge adjoining the Cengia Martini (which extends to the right – suitable for further exploration, experienced walkers only). The main route proceeds left via a snow-choked gully and final short tunnel, from which you take a steep scramble and zigzag path to join path n.402 for the final drop to **Passo Falzarego**.

Alternative descent via Rif. Scotoni (1hr 30min) to Sarè (1hr)

Return to the signed **2660m junction** below the refuge, and take n.20 (or Alta Via 1) north across the vast undulating incline towards **Lago di Lagazuoi** (2182m). The same number path drops north-northwest the short distance to **Rif. Scotoni** (1985m), on a winter ski piste. A small chapel nearby is the sole reminder of the erstwhile war cemetery here.

A jeep track leads the rest of the way down into a wooded pasture basin beneath the mass of the Cunturines and to pleasant bar-restaurant **Capanna Alpina** (1726m). It is then a mere 15min via the track to the road, where you turn left across the bridge for the bus stop at **Sarè** (1652m) for the return to Passo Falzarego.

In the WWI mountainside tunnel on Lagazuoi

Tourist Office Cortina d'Ampezzo
tel. 0436-3231/3232

Rif. Lagazuoi
tel. 0436-867303
private, sleeps 75,
open 20/6–10/10

Rif. Scotoni
tel. 0471-847330
private, sleeps 19,
open 24/6–30/9

19 – Settsass Circuit

Dwarfed into relative insignificance by the outstanding Dolomite massifs of Lagazuoi and Cunturines, the Settsass stands isolated, a jagged ridge rising out of gently rolling pasture. However it rates as one of the most amazingly panoramic formations with an easily reachable summit, Setsas – the variant spelling distinguishes the western peak from the Settsass group as a whole. The denomination refers to seven stones, though there are many more in actual fact.

Walking time	5hr 30min
Walk distance	13.5km/8.3 miles
Difficulty	Grade 2
Ascent/descent	730m/730m
Map	Tabacco n.07 scale 1:25,000
Start point	Passo di Valparola

Reaching a maximum of 2575m above sea level from a base that clocks in at 2100m, the Settsass group stretches in a west–east curve for about 3km. The northern aspect is a vast gentle slab-like incline, while the southern side declines abruptly with a series of magnificent walls and towers.

Settsass gained acclaim through the work of German palaeontologists, then geologists, in search of the key to unravelling the mystery of the formation of the Dolomites. The most eminent was Baron Ferdinand von Richthofen, who published a ground-breaking treatise in 1860 suggesting that they originated as a coral reef. The key point was the later-named Richthofen Riff (reef), a modest separate formation on the southern side of the Settsass, whose exposed fossil-rich beds were the basis for the scholars' ideas. Also known as Piccolo Settsass, it was extensively tunnelled by the Austrian–German troops during the 1915–18 conflict, as it provided an excellent observatory. Otherwise the formation saw limited action during the First World War, considerably less than the sadly renowned Col di Lana to the south, whose summit was blown to pieces by an Italian mine in 1916, with heavy Austrian casualties.

This magnificent circuit rates very high on panoramas and guarantees a remarkable array of wild flowers, marmots and even chamois on the high rocky reaches, together with abundant waymarking and few other walkers. A straight 300m ascent is entailed for the western summit, however the rest of the route could hardly be described as level, the innumerable ups and downs making for tiring going. No shelter or refreshment points are passed, so go prepared. The route is equally feasible in the reverse direction, and timing is the same.

STAGE ONE: FROM PASSO DI VALPAROLA VIA VAL PUDRES AND 2240M JUNCTION (1HR 30MIN)

Behind the refuge, or modest hotel, at **Passo di Valparola** (2168m) is signposting for path n.24 and the Giro del Settsass (the Settsass circuit). It skirts the knoll sheltering the building, then coasts above a fenced lake and dips to a signed junction (10min) where you turn right. A gradual climb across grassy flowered flanks leads over west to a broad saddle then the northern flank, soon reaching **military ruins**. The slopes above feature simple crosses fashioned with old timbers and fortifications, and invite exploration. The views are already breathtaking, with the Cunturines due north flanking the Val Badia with Sas de Putia and the Puez-Odle, to the distant snow-capped Austrian Tyrol. Below is rich pasture dotted with Arolla pines. The path continues beneath M. Castello in an essentially western direction, the ground continually rising and dropping, and the rocky peaks of Settsass are soon seen.

The grassy basin (Val Pudres) is crossed, where your approach will undoubtedly be signalled by the alarm whistles of the sentinels of the marmot colony. The climb north leads to the signed **2240m junction**, where you turn left for 'Cima Setsas', leaving n.24 for the time being.

(To avoid the summit climb, turn right on n.24 for the Sella Les Pizades and the ensuing Pralongià turn-off, then pick up the route at Stage Three).

STAGE TWO: ASCENT TO SETSAS (45MIN) THEN DESCENT TO PRALONGIÀ TURN-OFF (45MIN)

Faint red/white waymarking leads southwest diagonally up the grass-rock flank carpeted with purple oxytropis to gain a **red earth crest** (2340m) and extraordinary views

Access to start point:
SAD coaches from Corvara/Kurvar in Val Badia/Gadertal (late June through to mid-Sept) stop at Passo di Valparola en route to Passo Falzarego. Otherwise there are July to mid-Sept links with Dolomiti Bus from Cortina (and occasionally Belluno via Andraz) to Passo Falzarego, from where it's 2km on foot.

Drivers from the Val Badia will need the turn-off at La Villa/Stern for Passo Falzarego, whereas from Cortina it's the SS 48, the continuation of which also climbs in tight curves via Andraz from the SS 203 and Alleghe.

For the alternative exit/access via Rif. Pralongià, the Piz Sorega chair lift from S. Cassiano operates July–Sept.

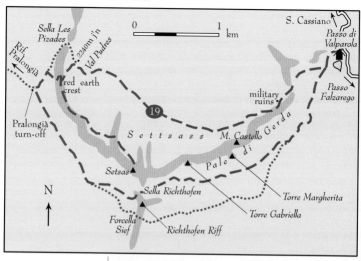

over the lush pastures of Pralongià to the Marmolada and its shrinking glacier, as well as of the Sella group. Marked by cairns, the path climbs southeast, keeping to the sloping northeastern side of the main ridge via a massive rock slab. You emerge at the western peak **Setsas** (2571m) and its single wooden cross on the plunging edge. As views go, suffice it to say that the Pale di San Martino, Civetta, Pelmo and dark brown Col di Lana of volcanic origin are included in the brilliant 360° vista. The Richthofen Riff is directly below.

• **An alternative access/exit route to S. Cassiano in Val Badia** runs via private Rif. Pralongià (1hr) then Piz Sorega (a further 1hr) and the chair lift to the valley floor.

From the peak, return the same way to the **red earth crest** (30min), and instead of bearing down right as per the ascent route, keep to the crest, where faint red/white paint marks lead easily down left to the western side, where path n.24 is soon joined, a short distance above the **Pralongià turn-off** (2200m, 15min from the crest). •

STAGE THREE: VIA SELLA RICHTHOFEN (1HR) AND PASSO DI VALPAROLA (1HR 30MIN)

It's southwest now on n.23 signed for Forcella Sief, past two picturesque old timber huts and onto rocky terrain beneath the Montagna della Corte, as this southern sector of the Settsass is known. Gradual ascent leads to several narrowish crumbly passages, where a sure step is recommended. About 45min on, below an evident saddle, search for the faint path leading up to the nearby saddle – it starts in the vicinity of faded lettering for 'Pralongià' painted on a rock.• 15min up is the **Sella Richthofen** or Forcella del Settsass (2360m), and those interested in fossil hunting and exploring the Richthofen Riff and its wartime constructions will enjoy this zone immensely.

The walk proceeds on a decent unnumbered path eastwards, dropping gradually then almost imperceptibly along the marvellous southern flanks beneath the Pale di Gerda and the impressive Torre Gabriella and Torre Margherita to eventually rejoin n.23 and the alternative.

As well as profusions of edelweiss on the open terrain, there are martagon lilies sheltering amongst the Arolla pines and dwarf mountain pines belonging to a wood which stretches out below with pasture clearings. A brief climb then a rock gully lead up north into a marshy muddy pasture basin with fluffy cotton grass, not to mention a number of wartime caverns and trenches, part of the Austrian 'Edelweiss' positions and supply line. The road and monumental Austrian fort are visible, and the path quickly reaches the junction with n.24 before returning to **Passo di Valparola** (2168m) and its hospitable hut.

•**Alternative via Forcella Sief**
Instead of climbing to Sella Richthofen an alternative, more straightforward, if marginally longer route keeps on lower n.23. It gains a grassy clay saddle with a crucifix, **Forcella Sief** (2262m, 20min), and from here a long series of ascents and descents leads around east to join the Sella Richthofen route.

Tourist Office S. Cassiano/St. Kassian tel. 0471-849422

Rif. Pralongià tel. 0471-836072 private, sleeps 25, open 27/6–end Sept

Rif. Valparola tel. 0436-866556 private, sleeps 30, open May–Oct

The western peak of Settsass

20 – Santa Croce Sanctuary

A monstrous fire-breathing dragon was terrorising the inhabitants of Val Badia, persistently demanding human victims. No shepherd or woodcutter dared venture out alone until the arrival of Gran Bracun (or Guglielmo Prack), a bold knight from Marebbe. Fresh from the Crusades in the Holy Land he wasted no time in pursuing the dreaded monster to its lair at the foot of the sheer rock face of Sasso della Croce and engaging in victorious combat.

Walking time	3hr 30min + 1hr 30min without chair lift
Walk distance	11km/6.8 miles
Difficulty	Grade 1–2
Ascent/descent	300m/800m + 500m without chair lift
Map	Tabacco n.07 scale 1:25,000
Start point	S. Croce chair lift at Pedraces

Nowadays, not far from the famed spot where the creature's bleached bones reputedly lay until very recent times, in spring and autumn processions of chanting villagers dressed in traditional garb visit an evocative high-altitude mountain sanctuary on pilgrimage. A separate mass is held for each hamlet, and prayer shifts start in the early hours of the morning. The sober white-washed church consecrated in 1484 holds a miraculous image of Christ bearing the cross, hence the name of the mountain – Sasso della Croce, 'stone of the cross'.

However an earlier chapel on the site was built in the 11th century when a wealthy count from the Val Pusteria withdrew in meditation here in repentance for his harsh treatment of his subjects. As that story goes, he donated all his earthly possessions to the nearby abbey, the *badia,* which gave its name to Val Badia. A chapel was planned in recognition of the pious act, but work was continually interrupted as the masons were unexplainably injured by pieces of flying stone. Imagine their amazement when gigantic white birds appeared to carry the bloodied chips up the mountainside and arrange them carefully on the site of the new building! The pilgrims' hospice (modern-day *ospizio*) building from 1718 was originally the sacristan's lodgings. Its inviting timber-lined premises now offer accommodation and delicious meals at very reasonable-prices.

The marvellously elongated Sasso della Croce, Sass dla Crusc for the Ladin-speaking population, resembles a crouching lion with massive haunches when seen from a distance, while Amelia Edwards (1873) likened it to 'a Cathedral with two short spires'.

The walk to the sanctuary makes use of a chair lift, saving a fair amount of climbing, before traversing a lovely wooded area at the eastern base of the mountain, returning to Pedraces via an easy surfaced farm road which is a little monotonous at times.

A welcome aspect of the final stretch is that it touches on a number of closely knit hamlets formed of clusters of ancient shingle-roofed timber farmhouses and barns, known as 'viles', namely settlement, probably from the Latin. Characteristic of Val Badia, they were grouped together for protection in medieval times, forming self-sufficient units with their own collective oven and well. Photographers and architects will have a field day. Surprisingly the space-age changes to the economy of the valley due to the advent of tourism and skiing appear to have passed these rural communities by, leaving them all but unaffected, with the exception of surfaced access roads. The properties have also been safeguarded from demolition and fragmentation thanks to the deeply rooted and legally recognised custom of the 'closed farm', introduced in the 6th century, whereby the eldest son is expected to carry on the farm activities and traditions, while siblings must leave to seek fortune elsewhere.

A direct exit for La Villa is also given in the walk, as well as an extension to San Cassiano, and you return by bus for both. An additional attraction of S. Cassiano is its modest museum, Pic Museo Ladin (tel. 0471-849505), which boasts the *Ursus spelaeus* cave bear skeleton discovered on the neighbouring Cunturines mountain, along with a good fossil collection and local artifacts.

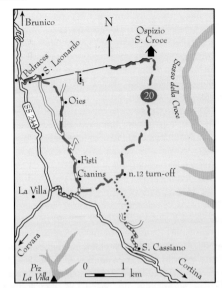

Access to start point:
Val Badia/Gadertal with the SS 244 runs south from Brunico/Bruneck in Val Pusteria/Pustertal, and is served by year-round SAD coaches. There are connections via all the main Dolomite passes in summer to Cortina, Val Gardena/Grödner Tal, Val di Fassa and through to Bolzano.

The modern chair lift used in Stage One operates from mid-June to early Oct. There is plenty of parking space at the chair lift station.

•**Alternative on foot to the upper chair lift station (1hr 30min)**
From the chair-lift departure point at **Pedraces** continue up the road to the picturesque hamlet of **S. Leonardo** (1365m) and its landmark 18th-century church. Path n.7 climbs through several old hamlets to the **upper chair lift station** (1840m).

STAGE ONE: ASCENT VIA CHAIR LIFT (15MIN) TO OSPIZIO S. CROCE (30MIN)

From **Pedraces** (1324m), 5min uphill from the bus stop on the main road, take the chair lift to the 1840m upper station (refreshment points).• Farm track n.7 doubles as a *via crucis*, and is lined with a number of huge crucifixes, not to mention handy benches in scenic spots. It ascends gradually eastwards through lovely conifer wood and flowered meadows. Ahead is the imposing face of Sasso della Croce, which turns a glowing fleshy pink as it catches the rays of the afternoon sun. It takes about half an hour to gain the simple but extraordinarily photogenic church and sanctuary of **Ospizio S. Croce** (Heiligkreuz Hospiz, 2045m). The position, at the foot of precipitous pale cliffs, is simply perfect. Directly across the valley is the spread-out Puez-Odle group, terminating in the Sass de Putia point to the northwest.

STAGE TWO: TRAVERSE TO N.12 TURN-OFF (1HR 15MIN)

Path n.15 moves off south into light wood and the realms of the Fanes-Sennes-Braies Nature Park, sticking fairly closely to the base of the mountain. Marked by more stations of the cross, it coasts through springy masses of dwarf mountain pines which shelter roe deer. Log walkways have been set up for crossing marshy tracts, colonised by fluffy cotton grass. The broad path drops gradually and there are several good lookout points over Val Badia and across to the Puez plateau with the Sassongher point. About 1hr 15min from the sanctuary you reach a clearly marked intersection – the **n.12 turn-off** (1743m). While the left branch climbs to Forcella Medesc, yours descends towards La Villa.

Extension to S. Cassiano (45min)

From the **n.12 turn-off**, keep south on n.15. In constant gradual descent it soon leaves the wood and crosses well-kept meadows to a huddle of farms followed by an old timber mill on the banks of a stream, still complete with its water wheel. After a series of modest ups and downs,

Ancient timber barn at Oies

a fenced-in stretch emerges on a narrow tarmac road. There are marvellous views of Piz dles Cunturines towering over the township, then magnificent Cima Scotoni and M. Cavallo and the Lagazuoi line-up not far away to the east. The road drops quickly, and just before entering the built-up zone you take a lane off left leading straight down to the new town centre. You come out between the church and the museum, virtually opposite the tourist office of **S. Cassiano** (1536m).

STAGE THREE: RETURN VIA CIANINS (30MIN) AND OIES (40MIN) TO PEDRACES (20MIN)

Path n.12 follows a watercourse dropping steadily through wood past one of many isolated farming hamlets amidst manicured meadows. Half an hour later you arrive at a surfaced farm road (1460m), where you turn right for the picturesque buildings of **Cianins** (1468m).•

The narrow road leads north via a string of hamlets, each with interesting houses, monumental barns and artistic crucifixes. A little way after the grouping at **Fisti**, a wider road is encountered. Keep left for a brief section downhill, then take the next branch right for the short climb to the sizeable settlement of **Oies** (1508m), venerated as the birth place of the 19th-century priest and missionary P.G. Freinademetz. Just after a panoramic coffee shop, a marked path leaves the asphalt to drop left, lined with stations of the cross. It leads down easily to **S. Leonardo** (1365m) and its late Baroque-style church with highly decorative stucco work. You then need the road which leads down to the chair-lift station and then to **Pedraces** (1324m) after a total of 1hr 30min from the n.12 turn-off.

• **Alternative exit to La Villa (10min)**
Keep left at the surfaced farm road (1460m) past Ciasa Sorëdl to join the road from S. Cassiano. Its two curves can be short-cut, then you cross the river for the nearby township of **La Villa** (1420m), with shops and bus stop.

Tourist Office La Villa/Stern
tel. 0471-847037

Tourist Office Pedraces/Pedratsches
tel. 0471-839695

Tourist Office S. Cassiano/St. Kassian
tel. 0471-849422

Ospizio S. Croce
tel. 0471-839632
private, sleeps 22,
open 10/6–10/10

21 – Puez-Odle: Sass de Putia Circuit

Walking time	6hr (4hr if the summit is excluded)
Walk distance	16.5km/10.3 miles
Difficulty	Grade 2 (Grade 3 for the final leg to the summit)
Ascent/descent	1070m/1070m (650m if the summit is excluded)
Map	Tabacco n.07 or n.30 scale 1:25,000
Start point	Passo delle Erbe

The views from the peak of Sass de Putia are amazing, as it is the most northerly of the Dolomites; what's more, it is claimed that a grand total of 449 church spires in the South Tyrol can be seen with a good pair of binoculars!

This stunning circuit walk takes in the ascent of magnificent 2875m Sass de Putia (or Peitlerkofel). This isolated mountain, the northernmost offshoot of the Puez-Odle group, has contrasting aspects depending on the approach. From the south it appears as a gentle grass-covered slope, while the northern aspect presents a series of impressive jagged peaks atop an abrupt 800m cliff, with a seemingly impossible summit point.

Passo delle Erbe, also known as Würzjoch, a reference to the grazing in the area, is located at the very foot

Sass de Putia, from Passo delle Erbe

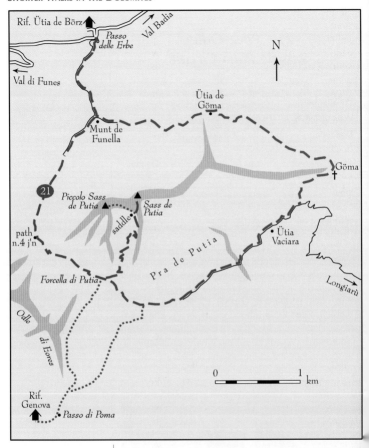

of the mountain and makes for a perfect start point. A hospitable refuge-cum-guesthouse with an excellent restaurant, Rif. Ütia de Börz, stands at the panoramic pass. The denomination Ütia, commonly found in this area, is the Ladin term for 'summer farm'.

Those keen on geology will find the environs of the pass especially interesting as the pale Dolomite formations of Sass de Putia rise from dramatic multi-coloured rock strata, mostly arenaceous material, exposed by the action of a watercourse. The road pass itself attracts a fair number of visitors in midsummer for its pleasant meadows and picturesque farms, though relatively few venture onto the paths. Then in low season it is all but deserted.

With the exception of the ascent to the summit, the circuit described here is of intermediate difficulty, well within the range of the average walker. The optional climb entails a steady 500m, the final 150m leg aided by a length of chain where it becomes steep and exposed. However, the latter is easily avoided by branching off west to an easier and only slighter lower crest, as explained in Stage Two. A number of modest huts turned refreshment points are encountered en route, most with marvellously scenic outdoor seating and farm-style eats. A detour is also feasible to popular Rif. Genova/ Schlüterhütte, though this adds a good 30min to the walk timing.

In addition, the village of San Martino in Badia, located on the eastern (Val Badia) side of the pass, is worth a visit for its newly renovated tower-cum-museum of Ladin traditions (tel. 0474-524020).

STAGE ONE: FROM PASSO DELLE ERBE TO FORCELLA DI PUTIA (1HR 20MIN)

Opposite the guesthouse at **Passo delle Erbe** (1978m), path n.8A/B strikes out south between two forestry tracks, past a modest restaurant and through a wood of Arolla pines. Close by is the edge of the depression where the dark red and grey strata underlying Sass de Putia are exposed. Heather and bilberry shrubs line the way as a wide track is joined past summer hay huts. Keep right at the signed junction (15min, 2067m) near the **Munt de Funella** hut to skirt the mountain southwest. The path narrows and alpenrose and dwarf mountain pine abound, while the views take in the impressive neighbouring Odle di Eores. Lengthy crumbly tracts and reinforced gullies bear witness to the succession of material deposited over time, and there are tiny shell fossils embedded in grey strata.

Access to start point:
Passo delle Erbe/ Würzjoch, a minor road pass, links upper Val Badia/Gadertal with Val di Funes/Villnößtal and Bressanone. The narrow 30km road makes for an extremely panoramic drive, though can be closed in the winter months by heavy snowfalls. SAD buses wend their way up here twice daily in summer from Val Badia via San Martino (late June to mid-Sept, except Sun and hols).

Some 50min from the pass, a broad gully is gained and path n.4 joined for a relentless 200m climb, zigzagging amongst strewn boulders, a trickling stream and Rhaetian poppies. The final leg is reinforced with timber traverses and steps, and more often than not is choked with snow in early summer. After all this barrenness, it comes as a genuine surprise to emerge at **Forcella di Putia** (Peitlerscharte, 2357m) and be confronted with rich rolling pasture land studded with rich yellow buttercups, gentians and pink mountain thrift.•

•Detour to Rif. Genova (50min)
From **Forcella di Putia** take path n.4 heading southwest on a level, and half an hour will see you at bustling well-placed **Rif. Genova**/Schlüterhütte at 2297m, close to Passo di Poma/Kreuzkofeljoch – a great place for lunch. Afterwards you'll need the wide path n.35 northeast in gentle descent to rejoin the main itinerary at a junction at 2140m (a further 20min).

Stage Two: ascent of Sass de Putia (2hr return)

Sharp left from **Forcella di Putia** is the path leading into the central fold of Sass de Putia, where a shallow gully-valley often harbours late-lying snow. Wide curves climb steadily – keep right at the fork around 2600m for a brief rock crest passage and ever-improving views. A broad **saddle** is reached at about 2760m (just under 1hr from the *forcella*). Here you have two choices. You can tackle the final cable-aided stretch via an exposed shoulder for the last 150m hands-on climb to the 2875m summit of **Sass de Putia**. Should that not appeal, turn left (west) at the saddle for the easy route to the twin peak, **Piccolo Sass de Putia**, only a matter of metres lower. 1hr 20min in all will cover the ascent, while a further 40min are needed back to the pass.

The views are quite amazing and range 360°, taking in a vast selection of Dolomites, from Sassolungo-Sassopiatto, the Pelmo, Civetta, Sesto group, Piz Boè on the Sella, as well as the northern snow-capped Austrian Alps. Tame alpine choughs keep you company.

Stage Three: via Göma (1hr 20min) then return to Passo delle Erbe (1hr 30min)

N.35 (signed for Göma) drops easily from **Forcella di Putia** down the pasture slopes which are home to marmots, and in about 20min is joined by the variant path from Rif. Genova (2140m junction), a rough farm track. A white gravel lane takes over as you head northeast through manicured pasture (Pra de Putia) past scattered old timber huts used at haymaking time. One of these, **Ütia Vaciara** (2025m), has been tastefully converted into a rustic eatery with a splendid outlook southeast over Val Badia to Sasso della Croce. In these open expanses chances are good of spotting soaring birds of prey. Soon afterwards is a signed junction – keep left, and not far diagonally uphill through light wood and flowered slopes is the minor pass known as **Göma** (2111m, 1hr 20min from Forcella di Putia), marked by a crucifix. The crest you are traversing is an eastern extension of Sass de Putia.

Next is a drop northwest on n.8A, with views all the way down to the village of Antermoia. The shady wood that follows provides shelter for both black grouse and capercaillie, attracted by the laden bilberry bushes in late summer. Pasture featuring tall purple gentians follows, then after a short stretch of dirt track you keep left via another inviting refreshment stop, **Ütia de Göma** (2025m). Due west now you are plunged into wood that has grown up amidst huge fallen boulders directly below the main peak, whose walls rise vertiginously overhead. The path climbs out back to pasture and the farm-cum-snack bar **Munt de Funella**, in the vicinity of the 2067m junction encountered in Stage One, where you turn right to return to **Passo delle Erbe** (1978m).

Tourist Office S. Martino in Badia/St. Martin in Thurn
tel. 0474-523175

Rif. Genova/ Schlüterhütte
tel. 0472-840132 CAI, sleeps 80, open end June to mid-Oct

Rif. Ütia de Börz (Passo delle Erbe)
tel. 0474-520066 private, sleeps 35, open 20/5–1/11

Sass de Putia seen from south, with the ascent paths visible

22 – Puez-Odle: Sentiero delle Odle

The Sentiero delle Odle or Adolf Munkel Weg is justifiably renowned as one of the most beautiful itineraries in the whole of the Dolomites. It skirts the base of the spectacular Odle group, whose perfectly suited Ladin name means 'needles'. Countless soaring spires and towers rise to dizzy heights above vast scree flows, whilst the valley flanks are cloaked with dense dark green forests of conifer. The path was named after the Dresden Alpine Club's founder and entails a delightful coast between the 1900m and 2000m mark, giving walkers ample time to drink in the marvellous scenery.

Walking time	5hr
Walk distance	16.5km/10.3 miles
Difficulty	Grade 2
Ascent/descent	950m/950m
Map	Tabacco n.05 and n.030 scale 1:25,000
Start point	Ranui

The Odle block off the head of Val di Funes, a particularly quiet rural valley. Its high altitude summer farms all occupy marvellous positions and supplement their income by serving meals and taking in guests, a real boon for visitors. Their cows, on the other hand, are left to roam far and free in pasture clearings up at the base of the mountains, and their melodious neck bells tell the young shepherds of their whereabouts.

Close to the start point, in the peaceful village of Ranui in upper Val di Funes, stands the much photographed church of St. Johann which dates back to 1744. A classical late Baroque style building with a characteristic onion-domed bell tower, it stands out against the dark green woodland and the marvellous backdrop of the pointed, teeth-like Odle peaks.

The walk described here follows forestry and farm tracks in the initial low areas, whilst clear paths through pasture, woods and across scree account for the high-altitude sections. In good weather there is no difficulty, though it rates average in combined terms of fatigue and duration. The route can be shortened by half an hour if you cut out Rif. Malga Brogles; however, that would be a pity. Moreover a descent via Gschnagenhardt Alm can be used as an emergency exit, but it means missing a substantial slice of the panoramic pathway. Lastly, the late afternoon bus can be used from Rif. Zannes down to the Ranui turn-off.

Midsummer walkers will need ample supplies of drinking water as well as sun protection, whilst cameras are recommended all the time. Autumn can be particularly stunning as the larch trees turn golden.

STAGE ONE: FROM RANUI TO RIF. MALGA BROGLES (2HR 15MIN)

From the modest hamlet of **Ranui** (1346m) amidst well-kept meadows, take the narrowing road (n.28) lined with hedgerows to the parking area and start of the forestry track, closed to unauthorised traffic. Not far along, after the branch for n.33 (the return path), you veer south and continue in shady wood via the valley floor alongside a minor stream, Kliefer Bach. About 20min more and you are pointed right across the watercourse for the start of a climb. Further up, cross back over the stream and the track comes to an end at a **1716m junction**. N.28 now starts labouring seriously upwards through light conifer wood rife with busy woodpeckers to emerge finally in pastureland. Quite close to the foot of the awe-inspiring Odle, at 1899m, turn right onto n.35 for the remaining 20min stretch to **Rif. Malga Brogles** (2045m). Occupying an idyllic spot carpeted with yellow button flowers early summer, this working dairy farm doubles as a simple *rifugio* and refreshment point for the many visitors who reach it from the Val Gardena side as well (see Walk 24). A playful St. Bernard makes a point of extending a warm welcome to newcomers.

STAGE TWO: TRAVERSE VIA SENTIERO DELLE ODLE AND 1993M JUNCTION (1HR 30MIN) THEN MALGA GLATSCH (15MIN)

From **Rif. Malga Brogles** backtrack to the **1899m junction** then proceed northeast on n.35. The light conifer wood of mostly larch and Arolla pine and pretty banks of pink alpenrose shelters timid roe deer. There are plenty of ups and downs and clearings for admiring the mountains. About 30min along is the fork uphill for Forcella Pana (which you ignore), followed by a drop into a clearing

Access to start point:
Val di Funes/Villnößtal is a minor side valley that branches off Val d'Isarco in the vicinity of Chiusa/Klausen. SAD buses provide it with permanent links with the outside world. The usual service terminates in the lower part of S. Maddalena, then it's a matter of 1.5km along the road to Ranui, where the walk starts. The occasional midsummer run (late June to mid-Sept) extends to Rif. Zannes.

Drivers can park a short distance uphill from Ranui.

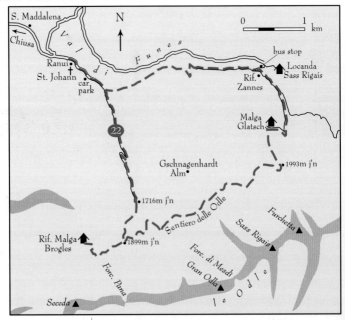

then spreads of dwarf mountain pines where the path becomes white gravel. Some time after a further turn-off (for Forcella di Mesdì, high above interminable tight zigzags via scree) an eroding earth ridge is climbed (2017m) and there are several forks for the unpronounceable Gschnagenhardt Alm not far below in a star-shaped clearing (a possible exit route). This point is directly beneath the prominent Sass Rigais, which reaches 3025m. On the ensuing stretch the path twists and turns to avoid fallen boulders and tracts where the scree flows have encroached on the path. Under the next easily recognisable tooth-like point, Furcheta ('fork'), is the key **1993m junction** where you leave the rocky realms of the Sentiero delle Odle and move into pastoral surrounds. **Malga Glatsch** (1902m), a quarter of an hour downhill, is a typical high-altitude summer farm, beautifully placed. The flowered meadows here in early summer are quite a sight.

STAGE THREE: DESCENT VIA RIF. ZANNES (20MIN) TO RANUI (40MIN)

A wide farm track (n.33) leads in leisurely curves down northwards to snack bar **Rif. Zannes** (1685m) and the car park and bus stop where the road from S. Maddalena terminates. Here you need forestry track n.33 due west on the southern edge of the Schwarzwald (Black Forest). Where the track bears left (south) a path breaks off straight ahead and soon hugs the banks of Rio di Funes, a delightful stroll. This leads back to the farm track taken at the start of the walk. Keep right for the short distance back to **Ranui** (1346m).

Church of St. Johann at Ranui, with the Odle

Tourist Office
Funes/Villnöß
tel. 0472-840180

Rif. Malga Brogles/
Brogles Alm private,
sleeps 32,
open July–Sept

Malga Glatsch/
Berggasthof Glatsch
Alm tel. 0472-840270
open start of June to
start of Oct

Locanda Sass Rigais/
Berggasthof Sass Rigais
tel. 0472-840133 open
late May to mid-Oct

23 – Puez-Odle: Roving Across the Altopiano

Bodies of water are a rare attraction in the Puez-Odle region, as phenomena resulting from karstification are widespread; this means that the rock surface is run through with deep fissures and clefts where the limestone has been dissolved by rainwater. Geology enthusiasts will find much of interest, as an unusually vast range of rock beds from successive past eras has been laid bare by erosion. Several volcanic-looking cones punctuate the central plateau, solitary remnants of the Jurassic and Cretaceous layers that once covered the whole area.

Walking time	5hr
Walk distance	14.4km/8.8 miles
Difficulty	Grade 2
Ascent/descent	500m/1150m
Map	Tabacco n.07 and 05 scale 1:25,000
Start point	Dantercepies gondola car, Selva

The rambling Puez-Odle group (also a nature park) that accounts for the mountains between Val Gardena and Val Badia offers a wealth of delightful walks on moderately easy terrain in dramatic landscapes. It is not as crowded as the neighbouring Sella group, thus improving your chances of seeing wildlife such as chamois and golden eagle, not to mention the multitudes of dragons that according to legend slumber in the depths of the scattered lakes.

This rewarding walk takes you into the very heart of the group via the elevated central plateau, which aver-

Passo Cir seen from Passo Crespeina

ages 2400m in altitude and hosts pasture basins smothered with wild flowers. A gondola car is used for the
initial 700m of ascent, and the route then proceeds in a
series of short climbs and descents before a final 800m
drop via the magnificent Vallunga. Sun protection gear is
recommended, as there is almost no shade except on the
very last leg. A manned hut, Rif. Puez, lies halfway and
is handy for lunch.

STAGE ONE: TO DANTERCEPIES (10MIN) AND PASSO CRESPEINA (1HR 15MIN)

Thanks to the **gondola car** at **Selva** (1560m), you are
transported in a scenic, leisurely manner up to
Dantercepies (2298m), overlooking dramatic Passo
Gardena. Take the vehicle track (signed for Sella Ronda)
east at first to the signed junction nearby for path n.2d,
which coasts the base of the Gran Cir amidst grassy
slopes thick with purple asters, bell flowers and gentians.
There are brilliant views from here across to the magnifi-
cent Sella massif, and east over to the Lagazuoi and
Tofane. A little further around is the former snack bar
Baita Clark (10min, 2222m), also accessible from Passo
Gardena. •

The path soon passes a sign announcing the border
of the Puez-Odle Nature Park and embarks on a steady
northeast climb through low-set dwarf mountain pines
and bleached rock. A silent inner valley of bizarre
knobbly rock pinnacles is soon gained, colonised by
yellow mountain avens. **Passo Cir** (40min, 2469m) means
a further short climb, and there are views down to Val
Gardena, not to mention the snowbound peaks to the
west. A sheep gate leads to a drop northeast (ignore the
turn-off for Selva) as you cut across the head of barren
Val de Chedul, where another brief ascent brings you out
at **Passo Crespeina** (15min, 2530m), with its evocative
sculpted crucifix. The marvellous views here take in the
Sciliar and Sassopiatto-Sassolungo to the southwest, the
distant Cevedale group beyond, and of course the vast
spread of the undulating innermost Puez plateau, punctuated by a number of unusual cones, vaguely
reminiscent of Monument Valley. Rif. Puez is visible due

Access to start point:
Selva/Wolkenstein is
located in upper Val
Gardena/Grödner Tal,
accessible by way of the
SS 242, which runs east
off the main Val
Isarco/Eisacktal at Ponte
Gardena/Waidbruck.
SAD buses from Bolzano
serve the valley year-
round, and there are also
links east with Passo
Gardena and beyond in
summer (late June to
mid-Sept).

The Dantercepies
cabinovia gondola lift
operates from late June
to late September.

•**Alternative access:**
It is feasible to slot into
the itinerary by starting
out at **Passo Gardena**
(2120m) and taking path
n.2 – an easy 20min
northwest as far as **Baita
Clark**.

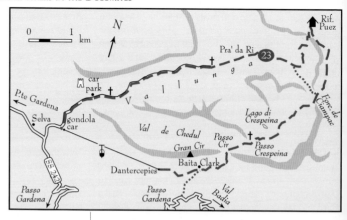

north, beyond the grazing slopes populated by chomping sheep.

STAGE TWO: VIA FORCELLA DE CIAMPAC (45MIN) THEN RIF. PUEZ (30MIN)

The path descends gently northeast and passes **Lago di Crespeina** (2374m), its shores perfect for leisurely daytime picnics. After nightfall, however, on enchanted evenings a halt is inadvisable due to the danger of flaming red mice that plunge into the waters, according to local lore!

The ensuing stretch traverses huge 45° tilted rock strata, en route to yet another pass, **Forcella de Ciampac** (45min, 2366m), where path n.4 from Colfosco joins up. (Here a variant path n.14 for Vallunga drops steeply left to negotiate a loose rubble gully, and necessitates a sure foot.) A brief rock corridor reinforced with timber treads leads north now over the plateau below one of the curious cones, Somafurcia, and traverses broad rock slabs embedded with a surprising number of fossilised Megalodont shells. Resembling cleft hoofprints of deer, these bivalve shells, averaging 10cm in length, date back some 220 million years.

You soon pass over the head of the magnificent Vallunga, a text book U-shaped glacially formed trough valley if ever there was one. Punta Santner and the Sciliar appear at its far extremity. Following the flag pole is welcoming **Rif. Puez** (30min, 2475m), backed by another strange green-red peak, Col de Puez. A restorative pause at the drinking fountain and some luscious Apfelstrudel are in order here.

STAGE THREE: DESCENT VIA VALLUNGA TO SELVA (2HR 30MIN)

Take n.14 (signposted for Selva) due south for the plunge into the **Vallunga** ('long valley'). The path is good, if steep at times, flanked by masses of felt-petalled edelweiss and

Glacially shaped Vallunga from the Puez altopiano

scrubby vegetation that anchors the loose terrain. Down at the bottom at a white rubble gully and stream (where the variant from Forcella de Ciampac joins up), you cross to the right-hand side of the valley below towering cliffs, the bulk of the descent behind you, and head west at first below a waterfall. Tree cover here consists mainly of dwarf mountain pines and larch. Not far along, the path traverses the beautiful pasture flat known as the **Pra' da Ri** (1hr 15min, 1800m), 'meadow for laughing', the site of merrymaking and fancy dress parties for the gentry of Selva in olden times.

A hut and crucifix mark the start of a *via crucis* with artistic stations which accompany the broad gravel track through light wood from here on (waymarking n.14). Further down keep left at the unmarked fork in the track, leading to a vast clearing and chapel. (Here you find the turn-off right to the ruins of Wolkenstein castle. Erected in the 1200s, it was short lived due to damaging rock falls. Only a couple of walls are left standing, though careful visitors can clamber up for a closer look.)

You eventually emerge near a **car park** and refreshment point (2hr 10min, 1650m). Keep straight ahead (left of the park) through to the Carabinieri training quarters and onto tarmac, where you go left past some houses, then left again at the intersection to return to the **gondola car** station at **Selva** (1560m).

Tourist Office
Selva/Wolkenstein
tel. 0471-795122

Berghaus Frara (Passo Gardena)
tel. 0471-795225
private, sleeps 30,
open 1/6–13/10

Hotel Cir (Passo Gardena)
tel. 0471-795127

Rif. Puez
tel. 0471-795365 CAI,
sleeps 90,
open 13/6–10/10

24 – Puez-Odle: Rasciesa and Geological Phenomena

Walking time	4hr 45min (reducible by 1hr excluding Rasciesa di Fuori)
Walk distance	17.5km/11 miles
Difficulty	Grade 1–2
Ascent/descent	150m/1000m
Map	Tabacco n.05 scale 1:25,000
Start point	main piazza, Ortisei

Artistic woodcarving has long been a mainstay in the burgeoning township of Ortisei/St. Ulrich in Val Gardena, 'the capital of Toyland' for Amelia Edwards who passed through in 1873 and left an account (right). It is also renowned as the birthplace of Luis Trenker, renowned mountaineer, actor and outstanding film-maker – English versions of two of his works were 'The Doomed Battalion' and 'The Challenge' from the 1930s.

Ortisei is dominated by the Rasciesa (often appearing on maps as Resciesa), a vast, gently sloping incline culminating in a jagged 2300m crest, and covered with rich pasture and woods of Arolla pine, the raw material for the wood carvers. Compared to its Dolomite neighbour, the stunning Odle group with pointed rock needles, it is unspectacular, but makes up for this in the wide-ranging views it affords. Rasciesa also acts as the dividing line between Ladin-speaking Val Gardena and German-speaking Val di Funes. The formation is easily accessible thanks to a chair lift that saves walkers 800m in ascent, and is popular with the locals for winter tobogganing.

The walk entails a panoramic traverse to a picturesque farm-cum-refuge, then a descent of great interest for geology enthusiasts as the multi-layered beds underlying the original coral deposits have been exposed on the westernmost edge of the Odle. The most ancient is a

'That remarkable animal on a little wheeled platform which we fondly took to represent a horse – black, with an eruption of scarlet discs upon his body, and a mane and tail derived from snippets of ancient fur-tippet – he is of the purest Grödner Thal breed. Those wooden-jointed dolls of all sizes, from babies half an inch in length to mothers of families two feet high, whose complexions always came off when we washed their faces – they are the Aborigines of the soil .... all these – all the cheap, familiar, absurd treasures of your earliest childhood and of mine – they all came, Reader, from St. Ulrich!'
(A. Edwards, 1873)

type of blood-red sandstone, rich in fossils, and which in 1969 yielded vertebra and bone fragments belonging to a porpoise-like Ichthyosaurus (probably Jurassic) at the foot of the Seceda mountain. It is overlaid by a multitude of grey-white chalks and grey-yellow layers dating back 240–250 million years. A wine-red porphyry from a later volcanic phase can also be seen further downhill. Special finds are on display at Ortisei's museum.

Good clear paths are followed at all times, with little climbing. The descent, while long, is not particularly steep, though it can be reduced by 630m and 1hr 30min by taking the lower section of the Seceda cable-car. Remember to be equipped for sun protection, as there is little shade on the Rasciesa crest. Late spring to early summer is the best time to visit for the explosion of wild flowers.

Access to start point:
The Val Gardena/
Grödner Tal and the SS
242 run east off the main
Val Isarco/Eisacktal at
Ponte Gardena/
Waidbruck. SAD buses
from Bolzano serve it
year-round, and there are
also links east with Passo
Gardena and beyond in
summer. The bus stop is
adjacent to the main
piazza in Ortisei, where
the walk starts.

The Rasciesa chair lift
functions June to mid-
Oct, while the gondola
car and cable-car to
Seceda run from early
June to early Oct.

STAGE ONE: ORTISEI TO RASCIESA DI FUORI (1HR) THEN RIF. MALGA BROGLES (1HR 30MIN)

From **Ortisei's** (1236m) main **piazza**, head uphill through the pedestrian zone past the tourist office and the elaborately decorated church, following signs for the Rasciesa **chair lift** (10min). The leisurely trip takes 15min up the vast forested slope, home to many a squawking nutcracker. At the **chair lift arrival** (2050m) and the bar/restaurant, you need the wide stony path n.35 west (signed for Rif. Rasciesa) across the grassy hillside carpeted with juniper shrubs and heather, where cows and chestnut Haflinger horses graze freely. **Rif. Rasciesa** (2165m) is only 20min away. Once there, take the path (n.31 at first) at the rear of the building leading uphill to the cross on the peak of **Rasciesa di Fuori**/Ausser Raschötz (2281m). Its isolated position is a guarantee of wide-reaching views in all directions: north over Val di Funes to the snowbound Austrian Alps, the Puez-Odle group to the east, and southeast/southwest Sella, Marmolada, Sassolungo-Sassopiatto, Catinaccio and Sciliar.

A clear but unmarked path now leads east along the crest then diagonally down to join the lower n.31 through pasture studded with fat gentians and black vanilla orchids. A good half an hour from the Rasciesa peak is a junction (2150m) and a link from the **chair lift arrival**. Hillsides wooded with Arolla pines and alpenrose shrubs thick with pink blooms characterise the stretch northwest

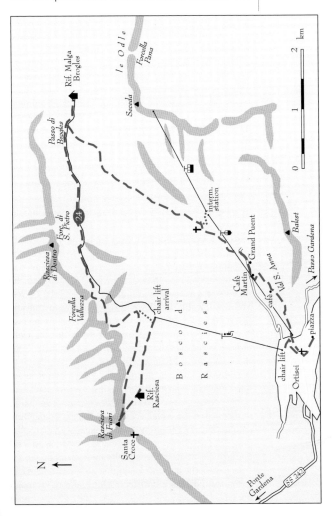

around to Forcella Valluzza/Flitze Scharte (2107m). Keep right for the wide track (n.36) that comes direct from the chair lift. It affords exceptional views of the Odle rock needles and scree flows, not to mention the massive Seceda point southeast with its exposed rock and earth layers.

From **Passo di Brogles**/Brogles Sattel (2119m) you drop briefly (east) to **Rif. Malga Brogles**/Brogles Alm (2045m). This summer farm, the stuff of picture postcards, doubles as a modest summer restaurant and simple refuge, and you'd be hard put to beat it as a lunch spot. (See Walk 22 for an itinerary this far from Val di Funes.)

STAGE TWO: DESCENT TO ORTISEI (2HR 15MIN)

Return to **Passo di Brogles** (2119m) and take path n.5 downhill southwest. It follows a stream then enters mixed conifer wood before taking a red earth-rock crest, with good views of the Seceda layers. Further down, it traverses the bed of the vast dry watercourse Cuecenes, not long before a signed junction and crucifix (1750m, 45min from the pass).

(At this point a branch leads left to the intermediate station of the cable-car, should you prefer to bail out here – 15min.)

Keep straight on through the wood (n.5), then below the cable-car to an old house and mill on a road (1495m). The ensuing tarmac drops through farms to cross a marvellous old timber bridge, **Grand Puent**, over a curious watercourse that has gouged a mini-canyon through a thick bed of red porphyry rock. At the nearby road junction and **Cafè Martin**, where you take the path signed for Val S. Anna, there are excellent views of more interesting layers on the Balest southeast across the valley. A steep drop brings you to a café-restaurant (1428m) ensconced in the wood. A clear track then a delightful path back and forth across a watercourse head gradually downhill past numerous picnic and play areas, as well as the arrival station of the ultra-modern gondola car, to emerge near the church. Continue straight downhill back to the main **piazza** of **Ortisei** (1236m), where the walk started.

Tourist Office Ortisei/
St. Ulrich
tel. 0471-796328

Rif. Malga Brogles/
Brogles Alm private,
sleeps 32,
open July–Sept

Rif. Rasciesa
tel. 0471-797186 CAI,
closed for long-term
renovation

25 – Alpe di Siusi: The Bulacia

Walking time	2hr
Walk distance	8.5km/5.2 miles
Difficulty	Grade 1
Ascent/descent	100m/300m
Map	Tabacco n.05 scale 1:25,000
Start point	Compaccio bus stop

Today the Bulacia serves winter skiers and summer strollers, and ensures a pleasant, varied and rewarding walk suitable for all, with the bonus of brilliant views. A series of manned huts-cum-restaurants is encountered for meals and refreshments, and a chair lift saves 300m in initial ascent. For the pedestrian alternative, allow 45min.

The Bulacia/Puflatsch is an apparently insignificant slab-like mountain sloping off northwards from the rolling high-altitude pasture plain of the Alpe di Siusi to culminate in a 2174m hummock. However, in the past, during the hysteria of the late Middle Ages, rumours were rife of witches congregating there and on the Sciliar, opposite. Even earlier it was documented as a lookout for Roman sentries, thanks to its bird's-eye observation possibilities.

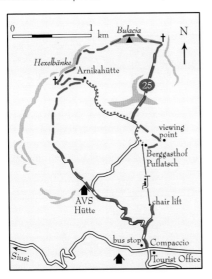

Access to start point:

Compaccio/Compatsch is served by year-round SAD buses from Bolzano and Val Gardena/ Grödner Tal. By car the Alpe di Siusi/Seiser Alm is well signed from both the Isarco/Eisack valley and Ortisei in Val Gardena. There is an ample fee-paying car park at Compaccio.

The Bulacia chair lift operates from the end of May through to late Oct.

STAGE ONE: FROM COMPACCIO VIA CHAIR LIFT (15MIN) TO BULACIA (30MIN)

From the bus stop near the nucleus of shops, banks and cafés at **Compaccio** (1835m), turn (north) up the road signed for the Bulacia/Puflatsch chair lift. You pass guest houses and branch right through a car park for a short descent to the start of the **chair lift** (10min). After the leisurely trip you are deposited at **Berggasthof Puflatsch** (2119m), a great scenic spot (though much more is promised!) and a good place to taste Holundersaft, elderberry flower juice.

Take the unmarked path right (due east) to a **viewing point** with helpful mountain profiles and name labels – quite stunning.

The path now proceeds in a northwesterly direction to join the lane labelled PU (turn right – north-northeast) ambling with gentle undulations. A good 20min from the viewing point will see you at the northeastern corner of the Alpe Bulacia and a **crucifix** in a breathtaking position. You find yourself on the brink of a vertiginous drop to the Val Gardena, backed by the Puez-Odle with the Seceda and the Rasciesa ridge. Dominating the visual southeast is the sliced-off shape of the Sassolungo-Sassopiatto group, flanked by the terraced Sella.

Next a path follows the cliff edge west above the thick Arolla pines which have somehow colonised the steep slope. The nearby 2174m peak of **Bulacia** is an almost imperceptible climb.

STAGE TWO: VIA ARNIKAHÜTTE (30MIN) AND AVS HÜTTE (30MIN) TO COMPACCIO (15MIN)

A little further on from the actual summit mound are the curious so-called **Hexelbänke**, which translates as 'witches' benches'. A minor phenomenon of volcanic origin and featuring augite porphyry, it has regular square-angled columns reminiscent of flagstones on the surface, whereas the exposed weathered blocks on the outer side are the actual benches, as legend would have it.

Still in the company of magnificent all-round views, press on in gentle descent through flowered grassy terrain that sports scented pinks and yellow mountain avens.

Keep left at the ensuing cross and signed fork (2059m, the right-hand path descends to Castelrotto) for **Arnikahütte** (2061m). (From here a lane leads left, south-west, back to the chair lift in 20min if needed.)

Turn right onto the AVS path for Compaccio. It skirts through low shrubs heading south, and makes for a magnificent walk. In the whereabouts of a copse of conifers, keep your eyes peeled for mini martagon lilies. After a farm lane and summer huts a rise is gained, and the AVS hut comes into sight. Either cut down the slope or stick to the ridge, which will lead you to a wider track leading to **AVS Hütte** (1950m), superbly placed opposite the Sciliar with a vast outlook stretching north to the snow-capped Austrian Alps. A broad track takes you back down to **Compaccio** (1835m) and the bus stop, where you started out from earlier.

Sassolungo-Sassopiatto seen from Bulacia

Tourist Office Alpe di Siusi/Seiser Alm
tel. 0471-727904

AVS Puflatsch Hütte
tel. 0471-727834 AVS,
sleeps 36, open all year

26 – Alpe di Siusi: Rif. Bolzano

Walking time	5hr 30min + 40min for ascent M. Pez
Walk distance	16.5km/10.3 miles
Difficulty	Grade 2
Ascent/descent	1000m/1000m + 113m for ascent M. Pez
Maps	Tabacco n.05 or 029 scale 1:25,000
Start point	Compaccio

The glorious Alpe di Siusi covers vast rolling meadows ranging from 1700m above sea level to around the 2000m mark, and even in this day and age continues to function as the haymaking arena for the village of Siusi, located at a much lower, more liveable altitude 1000m below. The Alpe is dominated by an ancient coral reef now known as the Sciliar/Schlern massif, at whose base volcanic intrusions have encouraged lush pasture carpeted with an unbelievable range of wild flowers, fed by plentiful natural springs or streams draining off the mountain. The very name, in fact, may signify 'flow of water', in view of the Schlernblut, a mysterious stream whose flow-level is constant all year round.

Carefully managed as the Parco Naturale dello Sciliar, encompassing 64km², this is a winter paradise for cross-country skiers and heaven for summer walkers. Only the odd farm vehicle necessary for supplies or haymaking is allowed up above the single road that connects Compaccio, the main arrival point, to Saltria at the eastern extremity, so you can wander in peace for days amongst dark timber farm chalets, many converted into picturesque refreshment points.

The walk, on clearly marked paths that undergo regular maintenance by park staff, is long but trouble-free in good weather, and understandably very popular in high season. Summer chair lifts such as the Spitzbühel and Panorama, as well as the marvellous environmentally friendly horse-drawn carts, can be used in Stage One as far as 1900–2000m, however you still have subsequent drops and climbs to deal with, so they don't really save much in terms of time and metres. Start out as early as possible because the ascent in the middle section can be hard going in fierce sun, and carry copious amounts of drinking water. Should you not opt for a panoramic picnic, the huts en route all serve light meals, snacks and all manner of drinks. Early summer visitors can expect to encounter late-lying snow on the

Sunset on M. Pez, with the Catinaccio

higher parts, though someone else will inevitably have trampled it beforehand.

STAGE ONE: TO SALTNERHÜTTE (1HR 15MIN)

At **Compaccio** (1835m), with its cluster of shops and hotels, you need the dirt road south, Straße Joch, between the main car park and the tourist office. It is signed as n.10, next to a board listing the huts ahead. After the first bend on a surfaced stretch, n.10 breaks off right and you shortly find yourself on a path crossing meadows south-southwest between old timber haymaking chalets. The occasional marshy tracts are equipped with plank walkways. Beethoven's Pastoral comes easily to mind as you catch sight of kerchiefed farm hands scything the sweet-scented hay. The snowbound Austrian Alps shimmer in the north, while the imposing Sciliar massif stands out to the west, with the great cleft Punta Santner, named after Johann Santer, a local mountaineer who was the first to scale it.

The path passes beneath cables for a winter lift, crosses a dirt track and drops to the strategic **n.10/n.5 junction** (1900m). Turn left down the lane (n.5), dipping into a basin with rich dark soil and past a fork for the Panorama chair lift. With the striking Terrarossa teeth-like points southeast, head through lush meadows past photogenic summer farms gay with pretty geraniums in window boxes to the **Saltnerhütte** (1850m). A madcap team runs this summer eatery, which is proudly advertised as the

Access to start point:
The turn-off for Alpe di Siusi/Seiser Alm is clearly signposted at Prato all'Isarco/Blumau in the principal Isarco valley, a short distance east of Bolzano. A further handy access road breaks off the Val Gardena. The final climb to the Alpe di Siusi can be found on the road linking the villages of Siusi/Seis and Castelrotto/Kastelruth. There is ample parking at Compaccio/Compatsch, the first settlement you reach, though fees tend to be hefty, and it is also served by year-round SAD buses from both the Bolzano and Val Gardena directions.

'letzte Tankstelle' ('last filling station') before the climb, with a 'blei frei' ('lead free') drinking fountain! The position is stunning, set against the easternmost extension of the Sciliar.

Stage Two: ascent to Rif. Bolzano (1hr 45min)

Suitably refreshed, continue on the wide Touristensteig ('tourists' path') n.5 across a stream, and start the 600m uphill section in the company of grazing cows and attractive red-tan Haflinger horses with blond manes. A little shade is provided by the thinning Arolla pines and lacy larch. Some 20min from the Saltnerhütte is a **1900m fork**, a key turn in the descent later for Proßliner Schwaige. After a breather to admire the views, you embark on a seemingly interminable series of steady zigzags, now waymarked n.1. The rock barrier is eventually climbed and the reward a magnificent undulating high-altitude plateau, the Altipiano dello Sciliar, with superb views of the neighbouring Catinaccio range and beyond. In pale stone, old fashioned **Rif. Bolzano** (2450m), dating back to 1885, has a marvellous glassed-in dining area and ranks high among the best-placed huts in the Dolomites.

Anyone with stamina to spare should head straight up the short climb to Monte Pez for even more breathtaking views. •

Stage Three: descent to 1900m fork (1hr), Proßliner Schwaige (30min) and Compaccio (1hr)

Retrace your steps downhill on path n.1 as per the ascent route as far as the **1900m fork**. Here turn off left, plunging into the lovely shady wood on path n.1A. Keep right at the ensuing branch, and not far off is a pretty waterfall then a watercourse surrounded by curious shows of green-blue shaley rock layers. Only minutes away is the delightful farm-cum-modest-summer-restaurant **Proßliner Schwaige** (1740m), a venue for rollicking live music, Tyrolian style.

Next climb up the steep farm track (n.10) northeast, and in a little over 10min an unmarked path breaks off left to follow a pretty crest which features hordes of tiny

---

• **Optional ascent: M. Pez (40min return)**
An easy 20min ascent takes you up 2563m M. Pez, an innocuous-looking hump north of the hut that reveals itself to be a lookout point *par excellence*, as well as being the culminating 'peak' of the Sciliar. The Sassolungo-Sassopiatto slants to the east; the Catinaccio, in all its pinnacled glory, lies to the southeast; the Latemar, aloof and majestic, is due south; and also visible are hosts of distant Dolomites. Archaeological finds of carbonised remains suggest that M. Pez was the site of animal sacrifices from prehistoric times right through to the Middle Ages, though local lore relates rumours of mysterious witches' Sabbaths, which led to the cold-blooded hunts in the 16th century (see Walk 27).

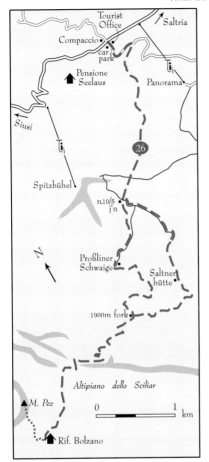

martagon lilies. This soon brings you out at the **n.10/n.5 junction** (1900m, 30min) mentioned in Stage One. From here you follow the same route used on the outward stage, and you should make it back to **Compaccio** (1835m) in another half an hour.

Tourist Office Alpe di Siusi/Seiser Alm
tel. 0471-727904

Rif. Bolzano/
Schlernhaus
tel. 0471-612024 CAI,
sleeps 120,
open June to early Oct

Pensione Seelaus
(Compaccio)
tel. 0471-727954

27 – Castello Presule

Walking time	2hr + 1hr castle visit
Walk distance	6.5/4 miles
Difficulty	Grade 1
Ascent/descent	85m/200m
Map	Tabacco n.029 scale 1:25,000
Start point	Fiè

Between 1506 and 1510, during the Counter-Reformation, a frenzy of witch-hunting overtook the small villages nestling at the foot of the monumental Sciliar massif. Two official figures, Knight Fuchs and Judge Lienard Peysser, were instrumental in condemning at least nine women in Fiè alone to death. The charges of evil deeds ranged from cohabitation with the devil, rain-making and riding on broomsticks to slaying unborn children and denial of the Catholic faith. 'Trials' in the castle of Presule were followed by torture and drawing and quartering, which reputedly took place at the artificial lake Laghetto di Fiè, brainchild of the castle's 16th-century proprietor, for whom it doubled as a fishing venue...

The castle of Presule is the destination on this walk, which consists of a delightful wander through meadows and charming farming communities occupying the vast slopes that climb up to meet the dark forested mountainsides and sheer bare rock of the Sciliar. The low altitude of the zone (800–900 metres above sea level) makes it feasible from spring through to autumn, with the castle a great attraction and a rare treat for the Dolomites region.

The earliest part of Castello Presule building dates back to the 1100s, but it was in the 1500s under Leonhard von Völs, governor of South Tyrol, that the medieval castle really took shape. It was fitted with an outer wall and a series of picturesque towers, state-of-the-art fortifications, a spacious courtyard, chapel, underground water storage, frescoed loggia, elegant living quarters with decorated timber ceilings, a great hall and a prison, access to which was one way – an 8m drop.

The last resident of the castle passed away in 1978, and luckily a consortium has since taken over to render the structure visitable. Exhibitions, concerts and private functions are held here in summer. Castello Presule/Schloss Prösels (tel. 0471-601062) is open for guided tours daily, except Saturday, from April through to October. Tours are conducted in German and Italian, though a summarised version in English is available on request.

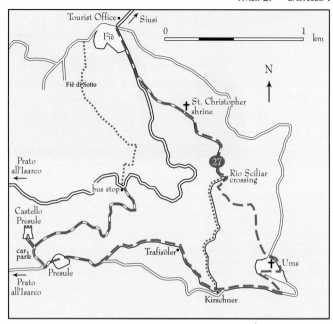

From the Tourist Office at **Fiè**/Völs (880m), in the shade of the Sciliar, follow the main road south-southeast in the direction of Bolzano, to where a quiet farm road, the Christophbildweg, turns off left (n.6). Soon the village of Presule comes into view to the south-southwest, its castle on an effective isolated outcrop in a commanding position. Passing orderly farms and apple orchards, you keep right at the fork for the unsurfaced lane past the **St. Christopher shrine** which gave the lane its name. Hedgerows and shady walnut and elder trees line the way. After a stream crossing (Rio Sciliar), turn right then take the left fork for the climb to Ums (whereas n.6 keeps straight on, a more direct route to the castle). A series of painted poles guide you past benches for the weary and through the fields to the village of **Ums** (935m, 45min).

Access to start point:
Fiè/Völs is served by frequent daily SAD buses 12 months a year on the Bolzano to Castelrotto/ Kastelruth line. By car from the main Isarco valley and the A22 autostrada, you need the Bolzano Nord exit then Prato all'Isarco/Blumau for the abrupt turn-off for Alpe di Siusi/Seiser Alm.

Castello Presule

Keep right past the church with a facade emblazoned with the figure of St. Martin, and around the corner for a lane left across a watercourse, where the road is rejoined for a short stretch due west (n.3). Down at **Kirschner**, a cluster of houses on the stream, the n.6 joins up, and a lane proceeds around the hillside past the hamlet of **Trafisöler** (847m). A curious square brick tower, the Pulverturm, is soon visible, originally built as a 12th-century guard tower. Tarmac leads through the modest settlement of **Presule** and down to a restaurant, then right at a junction for the car park and the photogenic structure of **Castello Presule** (856m), complete with picnic area and coffee shop.

• Alternative Return
For purists who wish to complete the walk on foot, from the bus stop take the lane under the road across the Schlernbach stream to reach the hamlet of **Fiè di Sotto**/Unter Völs, and from here follow a steep track back to the start point. This will take an extra 45min.

STAGE TWO: RETURN TO FIÈ (30MIN)
From **Castello Presule**, take the narrow road downhill in a northeasterly direction for the 2km descent to the main road and **bus stop** (20min) from which you take the bus for the return to **Fiè**.• A suggested follow-up is a cool beer at one of the old inns in the upper part of the village.

Tourist Office Fiè/Völs
tel. 0471-725047

28 – Circumnavigating the Sassolungo-Sassopiatto

Walking time	6hr 30min (5hr 45min via alternative)
Walk distance	18km/11.2 miles
Difficulty	Grade 2
Ascent/descent	850m/850m (1150m/550m via alternative)
Map	Tabacco n.05 scale 1:25,000
Start point	Rif. Passo Sella

'Then come the gigantic masses of the Platt Kogel and Lang Kofel; the first, sliced off, as by the malice of a Titan, at a single blow; the second, an array of splintered spires, ashy-tinted or pale yellow.'
(Gilbert and Churchill, 1864)

Gilbert and Churchill's quote refers to the unique Sassopiatto-Sassolungo ('flat stone' and 'long stone') formation, like Siamese twins joined at the midriff: however, one consists of a 45° inclined slab in contrast to a clutch of dramatic rock points and peaks. From the air it appears as a bleached volcanic crater open on one flank. It acts as the attractive centrepiece for this very promising day's walking in open terrain with a crazy kaleidoscope of amazing Dolomites shifting in focus all around. With an early start fit walkers will find it possible to walk around the entire block, though the multiple ups and downs on the middle section do make it a little tiring. However any one individual section makes for a wonderful walk in itself, with the help of the string of good huts with meals and shelter encountered at intervals of two hours at the most. The surrounds of Passo Sella can get quite crowded in midsummer, and the slopes are popular for picnics, so try and cover Stage One before the mid-morning peak hour. This initial tract around the 2200–2300m mark has been baptised the Friedrich August Weg. Ideated by the last King of Saxony, an expert mountaineer and keen Dolomite visitor, it follows ancient shepherd routes and offers a beautiful broad pathway with spectacular views. In sharp contrast the inner part

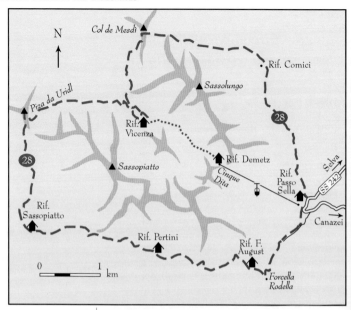

of the Sassolungo, where the going becomes marginally more difficult, is much quieter, and you might even get the return path to yourself.

When you stand at Passo Sella and look at the group, it is not hard to imagine the northernmost block as a massive head and the points left of the pass as a huge hand known as the Cinque Dita ('five fingers'). In legendary times the area was peopled by giants, kind-hearted generous creatures. But there was one exception, a scoundrel whose thieving habits earned him punishment and burial in the ground up to his neck with an uplifted hand, palm and five fingers held open to show it was empty. An even more dramatic story has a wicked king interred live under the rock, his desperate cries carried through the mountain by the wind. On a more 'domestic' level, the Bregostane nymphs used to hang out their washing on the rock spires.

STAGE ONE: VIA FORCELLA RODELLA (30MIN) THEN RIF. SASSOPIATTO (1HR 30MIN)

From the vicinity of the gondola car near **Rif. Passo Sella** (2183m), cut south across the grassy flowered hillsides to avoid the road, and link up with the broad dirt track signed 4/594 which passes a number of huts and winter ski lifts. You'll find yourself climbing steadily past lazing cows to **Forcella Rodella** (2316m), close to the station, for a cable-car from Campitello in Val di Fassa. The marvellous views here – northwest to the terraces of the Sella massif, and southeast to the Marmolada and Gran Vernel – are a good excuse for taking a breather.

You head northwest now, past the nearby **Rif. Friedrich August** (2298m), named after the king, portrayed in a wonderfully carved wooden statue of excellent Val Gardena workmanship. Above to the north-northwest is the evocative Cinque Dita formation alongside the Forcella Sassolungo, its hut visible.

At the foot of rock pinnacles called after renowned mountaineers Grohmann and Innerkofler, the earth path coasts easily amongst gentians and fallen rocks past **Rif. Pertini** (2300m), named in memory of a popular President of Italy. Views are becoming more ample ahead, with the Catinaccio southwest and the adjacent Sciliar to the west – very exciting stuff.

Summer farms precede a grassy ridge and saddle at the base of the vast Sassopiatto slab slope, occupied by the popular and hospitable **Rif. Sassopiatto** (2300m), often the venue of impromptu choral renditions.

STAGE TWO: TO RIF. VICENZA (2HR)

With inspiring views over the spread of the pasture idyll Alpe di Siusi, backed by the Austrian Alps, path n.9 drops quickly down a dirt track, which you soon leave for path n.527 off right. Passing hay chalets and across thickly flowered hillsides, the route makes a traverse northwards to an eroded earth ridge and stile (**Piza da Uridl**, 2102m) for the lovely sight of the Sciliar then Puez-Odle range, northeast. Arolla pines punctuate the ensuing 200m drop and junction with n.525 from S. Cristina in Val Gardena. Relentless zigzags then lead up into the inner realms of

Access to start point:
Passo Sella stands at the head of both Val di Fassa and Val Gardena, and the SS 242 climbs in countless zigzags from Canazei in the south or Selva in the north. There are also connections to Passo Gardena and Passo Pordoi. Passo Sella is served by a number of SAD coaches late June to mid-September.

The gondola car from Passo Sella to Forcella Sassolungo, useful for the alternative return, operates approximately from mid-June to early October.

the Sassopiatto-Sassolungo amidst blindingly bleached scree and astonishing clumps of Rhaetian poppies.

(If time is tight you can save a good 30min by skipping Rif. Vicenza and slotting straight into n.526 where it branches off left, north, for Passo Sella.)

The attractive stone building **Rif. Vicenza** (2253m), well camouflaged in the rocky landscape, is eventually reached. Although it looks out north over Val Gardena, the predominant feeling is very much of the towering, almost suffocating peaks – an awesome setting.•

STAGE THREE: VIA RIF. COMICI (1HR 30MIN) THEN PASSO SELLA (1HR)

This quieter route departs **Rif. Vicenza** by dropping some 15min to where n.526 forks off north signed for Passo Sella (note that a tempting higher path is narrower and

•Alternative exit via Rif. Demetz (1hr 30min) then gondola car (15min)
This slightly shorter return route entails a further 400m ascent on n.525 via a mysterious silent rock gully which harbours snow well into the summer. Sheer rock walls and towers dwarf walkers en route to **Rif. Demetz** (2681m) at the narrow opening, Forcella del Sassolungo, for the descent via the gondola car to **Passo Sella**, unless you opt for the steep knee-jarring descent on scree (allow 45min extra).

The King of Saxony on the Friedrich August Weg

View of Sassolungo-Sassopiatto from the Viel del Pan

Tourist Office Canazei
tel. 0462/601113

Tourist Office
Selva/Wolkenstein
tel. 0471-795122

Rif. T. Demetz
tel. 0471-795050
private, sleeps 26,
open 16/6–late Sept

subject to rock falls). A mostly level stretch leads to a crumbly crest (**Col de Mesdì**) and soon afterwards is joined by a path from S. Cristina. At this stage the path has become n.526a, and now leads due east for **Rif. Comici** (2153m), a refreshment point with an exceptional panorama over to the Sella group. Now it's a leisurely coast southwards as you close the circuit, passing through the marvellous unearthly landscape of tumbled boulders, an ancient rockfall from the Sassolungo, dubbed Città dei Sassi ('city of the stones'), to emerge at **Rif. Passo Sella** (2183m) once more.

Rif. Friedrich August
tel. 0462-764919
private, sleeps 55,
open year-round

Rif. Passo Sella
tel. 0471-795136 CAI,
sleeps 80,
open 15/6–end Sept

Rif. Pertini
tel. 0462-750045
private, sleeps 9,
open 20/6–20/9

Rif. Sassopiatto
tel. 0462-601721
private, sleeps 50,
open 15/6–10/10

Rif. Vicenza
tel. 0471-792323 CAI,
sleeps 40,
open 15/6-20/9

29 – Sella: Piz Boè Circuit

Walking time	4hr 30min + 1hr 20min if cable-car not used
Walk distance	8.5km/5.3 miles
Difficulty	Grade 3
Ascent/descent	370m/1100m + 590m ascent without the cable-car
Map	Tabacco n.07 or 05 scale 1:25,000
Start point	Passo Pordoi

The massive terraces cleft by profound gullies and soaring dolomite towers of the colossal Sella group are visible from afar. Its isolated fortress structure, bounded by plunging rock walls, make it an outstanding landmark, instantly recognisable. The high reaches resemble lunar terrain, awe-inspiring to say the least, though not exactly inviting for walkers at first sight. There is not a tree to be seen, though there is no lack of vegetation in the shape of lichens and hardy, brightly-coloured, ground-hugging wild flowers. The rock itself holds a treasure trove of fossilised ammonite shells.

An excellent network of paths traverses the massif, aided by cable-cars that take the sting out of the steep approaches from the four strategic road passes around the Sella. Wind-swept and snowbound for an extended season, the group boasts a 3152m pyramidal peak, Piz Boè, of relatively straightforward access in optimum conditions: usually midsummer or early autumn, and preferably with perfect visibility. Undoubtedly the most dramatic lookout peak accessible by walkers in the Dolomites, it is the highest point reached in this guide.

The walk rates as fairly difficult due to a couple of aided stretches on the climb to the summit, then a tricky steep gully during the ensuing descent in Stage Three, where masses of unstable rubble are often overlaid with icy snow well into the walking season. There are also some exposed stretches on the final return path to the pass. Some experience and care is recommended, and good weather is essential. The height gain and loss involved make for a somewhat tiring walk. Clothing for extreme conditions should be carried, as the massif is exposed and weather conditions often change unexpectedly, and don't forget high-grade sun protection cream and hat as well. The Sella group is justifiably a very popular destination in August making July or September the most suitable months.

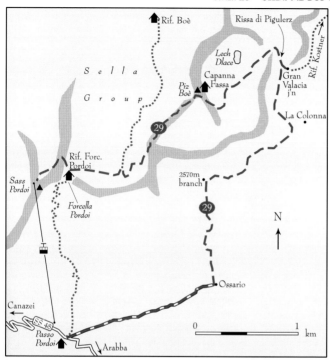

An easier (Grade 1–2) alternative route is feasible from the cable-car on Sass Pordoi via Forcella Pordoi and across to Rif. Boè – return the same way. It entails minimal height gain and loss and 2hr return timing. Moreover the main walk can be transformed into a rewarding traverse by extending via Rif. Kostner then Corvara (see Stage Three).

STAGE ONE: FROM PASSO PORDOI VIA SASS PORDOI (10MIN) TO FORCELLA PORDOI (10MIN)

The cable-car from **Passo Pordoi** (2239m) whisks you up to **Sass Pordoi** at 2950m in a matter of minutes. Perched on this corner of the gigantic Sella, you get stunning views of the Catinaccio to the west-southwest, the Sciliar

Access to start point:
The SS 48 leads to Passo Pordoi, which lies between Val di Fassa and Arabba at the head of the Val Cordevole.

The SAD bus company connects Passo Pordoi with Canazei, Passo Sella and Arabba from late June to mid-September, while the cable-car usually operates from late June to late September.

(west) and Sassolungo-Sassopiatto (adjacent west), not to mention the stark bare plateau of the Altopiano delle Meisules to the north on the Sella itself and, close by, the bizarre form of Piz Ciavazes, a mountain atop a mountain. The overwhelming sense is of a stone desert, but with towering natural structures instead of a flat expanse. Optimistic crows wheel overhead, on the lookout for tourists' scraps.

Once you've taken all that in, make your way past the classy restaurant, Rif. Maria, and northeast (with everyone else) for the brief descent across bare rock marked with cairns to the narrow opening **Forcella Pordoi** (2829m), which shelters a welcoming private refuge, **Rif. Forcella Pordoi.•**

•Alternative path to Forcella Pordoi (1hr 40min)

On foot from **Passo Pordoi** path n.627 (also marked Alta Via 2) climbs steadily due north across grassy terrain then zigzags up scree in view of the dangling cable-car. The last leg towards the rock opening of the pass hugs the cliff, the steep gradient helped by a cable and brief flight of steps. Icy snow is common in early summer. This 600m climb takes you into the inner world of the Sella at **Forcella Pordoi** (1829m).

STAGE TWO: ASCENT PIZ BOÈ (1HR 10MIN)

From **Forcella Pordoi** path n.627 proceeds due east via a broad natural ledge through a landscape of white-yellow-grey rock. At the ensuing fork keep right on n.638 (left, n.637, leads to Rif. Boè, 45min away on mostly level ground at 2871m). You climb gradually in a northeasterly direction traversing a series of rock platforms prior to a steep stretch which involves several hands-on sections – namely the southwest crest of Piz Boè – but nothing particularly difficult or exposed in good conditions. All effort is amply rewarded both en route and on arrival at breathtaking **Piz Boè** (3152m) and its modern hut, Capanna Fassa, along with a huge repeater. An unbeatable spot with wide-ranging panoramas.

STAGE THREE: DESCENT VIA GRAN VALACIA JUNCTION (1HR 10MIN), OSSARIO (1HR 20MIN) THEN PASSO PORDOI (30MIN)

The descent route, n.638 (Corvara painted in black lettering), wastes no time in dropping in a broad curve, southeast at first, then northeast. A good path, it offers sweeping views north over Val Badia to Sasso della Croce and the Cunturines group, Lagazuoi and, of course, the Marmolada to the southeast. A steady descent will see you traverse a flatter basin that houses the Lech Dlace

Piz Ciavazes on the Sella, from Sass Pordoi

(2833m), or the 'iced lake', though it doesn't exactly stand out, before reaching the head of an abrupt rubble-choked gully (45min). Under the curious denomination of **Rissa di Pigulerz**, Ladin for ravine and sheep herders, it needs negotiating with a sure step, and could harbour hardened snow even in summer. Be careful not to dislodge loose stones as there may be other walkers below. Red paint splashes show the best way down.

At the bottom is the **Gran Valacia junction** (2620m), with an extraordinary ample basin. Turn right here on n.626, due south. (The left branch, n.638, proceeds north via Rif. Kostner and a chair lift then gondola car for Corvara – 1hr 20min from this junction.) The way narrows quickly and follows a series of ledges hugging the Sella's southwestern flank. It enters a desolate realm of chaotic toppled rocks beneath sheer towering cliffs with overhangs that dwarf the few human figures who come this way. There are continual ups and downs and tiring clambers, not to mention several fairly exposed tracts, but the rewards come in the form of nimble chamois and plentiful wild blooms, such as king-of-the-Alps and pretty pink cinquefoil. Once a prominent point (near **La**

Piz Boè with Capanna Fassa

Tourist Office Arabba tel. 0436-79130

Rif. Boè tel. 0471-847303 CAI-SAT, sleeps 70, open 20/6–30/9

Capanna Fassa tel. 0462-601723 private, sleeps 20, open 20/6–20/9

Rif. Forcella Pordoi tel. 0368-3557505 private, sleeps 8, open 20/6–20/9

Rif. F. Kostner cell tel. 368-277954 CAI, sleeps 28, open 20/6–30/9

Casa Alpina (Passo Pordoi) tel. 0462-601279, sleeps 45, open June to mid-Oct

Colonna) has been rounded, Arabba and the Passo Pordoi road come into view, backed by the volcanic Padon chain. Some 40min from the Gran Valacia junction the turn-off upwards for the Ferrata Piazzatta is passed, followed by a grassy basin and a **2570m branch** sharp left marked with orange paint dots in the direction of the circular Ossario building, directly below.

This unnumbered path winds easily downwards via pleasantly flowered slopes of gentians and edelweiss, rife with marmot burrows. It emerges at the **Ossario** (2229m) or Sacrario, a stark military mausoleum that contains the remains of 8000 German and Austrian soldiers from the First World War along with 800 from the Second, all of whom perished in the vicinity.

A quiet surfaced lane leads back to **Passo Pordoi** (30min).

30 – The Sass d'Adam Crest

Walking time	2hr 45min + extra if lifts not used
Walk distance	7km/4.3 miles
Difficulty	Grade 2
Ascent/descent	350m/450m + extra if lifts not used
Map	Tabacco n.06 scale 1:25,000
Start point	Ciampac cable-car, 1km from Alba

The walk can be done in a half-day, as lifts are used at both the start and finish, though on-foot alternatives are always possible. Straightforward, clear paths marked with red and white paint stripes are followed, the only difficulty being encountered on the central section, which is narrow and a little slippery in wet conditions. However, as the main attraction of the itinerary is its great scenic appeal, it wouldn't be worth undertaking it in bad weather.

STAGE ONE: CABLE-CAR TO CIAMPAC (10MIN) THEN PATH TO SELLA BRUNEC (50MIN)

By cable-car (1486m) it is a breathtaking trip to **Ciampac** (2160m), an ample grassy basin bounded by dark volcanic formations: northwest is Crepa Neigra, suitably named for its colouring of volcanic origin, facing the towering Colac (southeast). The area is dotted with pylons for winter ski lifts, but they don't detract from the stunning views over to the unmistakable magnificent Sella group (north), with Sass Pordoi and Piz Boè, preceded by the dark Padon chain.

Alternative on foot from Alba to Ciampac (2hr)

From the village of **Alba** (1517m), wide track n.644 climbs the heavily wooded mountainsides steadily south. It passes under the cable-car on the final stretch to **Ciampac** (2160m).

An extensive zone in upper Val di Fassa consists of blackened terrain, in striking contrast to resplendent neighbouring Dolomite groups. Way back in geological time, as coral beds and marine debris were being deposited in shallow tropical seas, underwater volcanoes were simultaneously issuing streams of red hot lava. These broke through the pale surface layers and left a heritage of dark rock. A drawn-out process of hardening, uplifting and erosion produced the modest formations seen today such as the Sass d'Adam, rare metamorphic islands in a sea of pale sedimentary dolomite. Geology buffs will be fascinated by the minerals such as amethyst, prehnite and heulandite, while a boon for walkers are the vast panoramas and bounty of wild blooms that accompany the path.

Access to start point:

Val di Fassa can be reached from many directions, the easiest of which is probably the SS 48, which leaves the main Trento-Bolzano valley at Ora and transits via the Val di Fiemme. Atesina buses from Trento (mid-June through to mid-September) serve both Pozza di Fassa and Alba.

The Ciampac cable-car (27/6–14/9), used for the initial ascent, is located 1km from Alba along the road towards Penia. There is also a higher chair lift to Sella Brunec, but the short range limits its usefulness; it can be counted on from 10/7 to 31/8. The Buffaurè gondola car for the descent operates 20/6–28/9.

A broad track (n.644) moves off past Rif. Tobià del Giacher, in lieu of the Brunec chair lift, and starts the gentle climb southeast across flowered meadows up the middle of the valley. Several drinking-water points are encountered. The clear saddle **Sella Brunec** (2428m) offers more brilliant views: Sasso delle Croce has now appeared beyond the Padon chain, while snowbound Punta Penia on the Marmolada can be seen due east. Ahead (west) is the extraordinary spectacle of the Catinaccio-Antermoia massifs and the Latemar, while yet further beyond is the Ortles group.

STAGE TWO: VIA SASS D'ADAM (30MIN) TO BUFFAURÈ (1HR), DESCENT TO POZZA DI FASSA (15MIN)

Ignore the branch for the descent via Val Giumella to Pozza, and stick to n.613. After a brief drop the narrow path climbs to a crest below **Sass Porcel**, where marmots might show themselves. Soon there are dizzy views to Val San Nicolò, below south. The panorama also takes in Sassopiatto-Sassolungo to the north, and closer at hand are thriving alpenrose and bilberry shrubs. A gentle climb with some exposed tracts which could be slippery when wet is brightened by rock crannies which shelter tiny forget-me-nots and cactus-like stonecrop. Keen eyes will be able to pick out brick-red crystals of heulandite here. The next compulsory stop is at **Sass d'Adam** (or Sass de Dama, 2430m), with its unbeatable 360° views.

Ciampac backed by the Sella

A little further on (15min) you reach a **Punto Panoramico** and bench on Pala del Gaigher (2372m), where a sign declares that a good 16 alpine refuges are visible. Out with those binoculars again! The route heads south now, facing the Costabella and Monzoni chain, not to mention Sasso delle Undici, and zigzags down the grassy Valvacin slopes to old timber huts and a **2226m junction**, where a path breaks off for Sauch in pretty Val S. Nicolò. Keep right (west) via pastoral slopes. A wide farm track is soon joined past an impressive wall of solidified lava bubbles, then the fork to homely Rif. Buffaurè (2043m). The departure of the **Buffaurè** gondola lift (2044m) is only a matter of minutes away now.

The modern cabins glide over a pine forest to deposit you near the village of **Meida**. Then it's a short walk down to the main road and **Pozza di Fassa** (1304m), where you can catch a bus back to Alba.•

•**Alternative descent on foot (1hr 20min)**
From Rif. Buffaurè path n.643, a wide track at first, leads in a vast curve down to Meida and the road for **Pozza di Fassa**.

Tourist Office Alba di Canazei
tel. 0462/601354

Tourist Office Pozza di Fassa
tel. 0462-764117

Rif. Buffaurè
tel. 0462/764101
private, sleeps 20,
open 20/6–28/9

Rif. Tobià del Giacher (Ciampac)
tel. 0462-602385
private, sleeps 15,
open 27/6–14/9

31 – Marmolada: Rif. Falier

Gilbert and Churchill (1864) effected an excursion up the valley: 'It is a mere cup hoisted up upon the side of the Marmolata and at such a height that the south precipice which drops into it, loses much of its expected effect. If the Ombretta had lain as deep as we supposed, then that precipice must have been prodigious .... On the side opposite the Marmolata rise dark snow-patched rocks, and the whole boulder-sprinkled hollow is a perfect specimen of dreariness.' Go and judge for yourself!

Walking time	3hr 40min (2hr 40min wth a car)
Walk distance	12.5km/7.8 miles
Difficulty	Grade 1–2
Ascent/descent	700m/700m
Map	Tabacco n.015 scale 1:25,000
Start point	Malga Ciapela

This is a straightforward itinerary behind the impressive rock wall of the 3342m Marmolada, the highest point in the Dolomites. The mountain is renowned for a sprawling and rapidly shrinking glacier on the northern face, as a winter and summer ski playground complete with breathtaking cable-cars, and also as a theatre of extended hostilities during the First World War (see Walk 32). This route follows the Valle Ombretta, 'valley of shade', so-named for the proximity of the Marmolada as well as towering Sasso Vernale, an imposing barrier that makes up the western extremity with Cime Ombretta.

The walk is suitable for family groups, though probably not as a first walk in view of the 700m height gain it entails. Plenty of frolicking marmots are guaranteed, as a vast colony inhabits the middle section of the valley, while walkers with a keen eye may even spot the magnificent ibex way above Rif. Falier, which is a recommended spot for lunch.

After the walk, a worthwhile digression leads to the nearby Serrai di Sottoguda, east of the start point. Malga Ciapela once stood on the edge of an ancient lake whose downstream outlet sculpted a massive canyon, well over 100m deep. The old road winds some 2.5km through the depths of the Serrai, dialect for 'closed', while the trafficked new road sticks to a high route and crosses the gorge via a spectacular bridge.

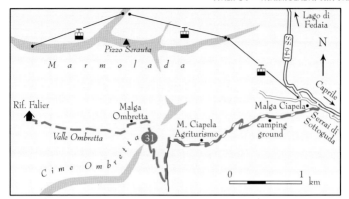

Stage One: to Malga Ciapela Agriturismo (30min)

Just south below the small-scale ski resort of **Malga Ciapela** (1384m), take the narrow road (signed n.610) west alongside Torrente Pettorina watercourse and past a camping ground. It climbs steadily through thick forest to reach pasture clearings and the well-established farm **Malga Ciapela Agriturismo** (1534m). In addition to appetising meals, fresh butter, cream and ricotta cheese are on sale.

Stage Two: via Malga Ombretta (1hr) then Rif. Falier (30min)

Soon after the **Agriturismo** and car park the asphalt comes to an end and the uphill section starts in earnest. Keep right at first, though you're advised not to take the signed *scorciatoia* (short cut), as it entails a pretty steep path. The main route for Rif. Falier (a dirt track), climbs easily south initially (ignore turn-offs left), narrowing into a path northwest as you climb above the thinning wood. It passes close to a rock face covered with some exquisite blooms, such as the unusual devil's claw, prior to an ingenious cutting. You emerge into the vast silent grazing reaches of Valle Ombretta, inhabited by sheep and goats under the watchful eye of the shepherd from **Malga Ombretta** (1904m), directly below Pizzo Serauta on the

Access to start point:
Malga Ciapela is on the SS 641, which connects Caprile to Canazei in Val di Fassa, via Lago di Fedaia. Those with a car can drive all the way to the Malga Ciapela Agriturismo farm in Stage One, and cut 1hr off the total walk time.

Dolomiti Bus has a July–Sept line from Cencenighe to Malga Ciapela. Otherwise you can use the year-round service to the village of Sottoguda, then walk the 2.5km west via the Serrai di Sottoguda to Malga Ciapela.

161

southern flank of the Marmolada. Ahead the valley opens up, lined by breathtaking light coloured walls, and provides an inspiring backdrop for a picnic, with delicious fresh water available at a generous hiccupping fountain.

The clear path proceeds along the northern side of the valley, high above the pasture flat and watercourse. It cuts lush green hillsides dotted with wild flowers and pines, and punctuated with a gigantic 'H' for the emergency helicopter landing pad. This is the best stretch for observing the playful marmots, who will undoubtedly alert you to their presence through shrill warning cries.

Only half an hour of almost imperceptible ascent from the malga is **Rif. Falier** (2074m), an exemplary hut run by a friendly local family who have been bringing in supplies by backpack for years.

It affords some unforgettable views eastwards of the Civetta and Pelmo groups, which catch the golden rays of the setting sun. The hut was inaugurated in 1911, but the ensuing war left it in ruins. Reconstruction had to wait 22 years; however, once again hostilities intervened and it was not until 1948 that it could really function. The *rifugio* is a strategic base for climbers attempting the plethora of challenging routes on the marvellous Marmolada, as testified by the diagrams in the dining room. Directly above the building you can see the metallic building belonging to the top station of the multistage cable-car from Malga Ciapela.

Rif. Falier
tel. 0437-722005 CAI,
sleeps 48,
open 1/6–15/9

STAGE THREE: RETURN TO MALGA CIAPELA (1HR40MIN)

Return to **Malga Ciapela** the same way you came.

32 – Viel del Pan

Walking time	2hr
Walk distance	6.5km/4 miles
Difficulty	Grade 1–2
Ascent/descent	150m/350m
Map	Tabacco n.07 or 015 scale 1:25,000
Start point	Arabba

The Padon chain, a broad ridge of dark volcanic origin, runs east–west in stark contrast to the pale colours of the Dolomite-limestone mountain groups of the Sella and Marmolada it separates. The fertile earth, a rich chocolate brown, sustains a remarkable covering of wild flowers, and keen eyes will pick out an edelweiss or two among the multi-coloured blooms. It also ensures thick pasture cover for the flocks of sheep brought up to graze in the company of timid chamois, all apparently unperturbed by sheer cliff edges devoid of protective fencing.

The Viel del Pan makes for a highly recommended straighforward walk and affords excellent views of the glacier on the Marmolada. The latter, known as the Queen of the Dolomites due to its 3342m, consists of limestone. The earliest known attempt at exploration dates back to 1804 when a local priest, doctor and lawyer set out ostensibly on a quest to examine the nature of the glimmering sheet of ice and put an end to widespread superstitious beliefs. It was not until 1860, and John Ball and company, that Punta Rocca (3309m) was reached, followed in 1864 by Punta Penia, the highest point in the whole of the Dolomites, attained by Grohmann and the Dimai brothers, his guides.

The ownership of the glacier is currently being hotly contested by two provinces in view of its historical impor-

An age-old trade route, the Viel (or Vial) del Pan runs along the elongated spine of the Padon chain. In the late Middle Ages it was used by grain smugglers to avoid the heavy taxes imposed by the Venetian Republic, hence the reference to bread (pan) in the name. The path was restored by the German Alpine Club in the late 1800s and is also known as the Bindlweg, after the then president.

The Marmolada and its glittering glacier from the Viel del Pan

tance and, of course, the tourist dollar, as its year-round cable-cars spell skiing.

As regards the actual origin of the glacier ... in the not-too-distant past the cult of Our Lady of the Snow was in vogue even in far-flung hamlets in the Alps. It originated with an unusual August snowfall in fourth-century Rome, and became an important occasion for worship, processions and get-togethers in the high-altitude villages. One year, on a balmy summer's day on the lush, verdant slopes of the massive Marmolada mountain, as the other peasants were heading valleywards to pay homage to the Virgin and invoke protection for the coming year, one ageing peasant woman stayed back to rake in the hay as the weather appeared to be turning bad. Heedless of the admonitions from her companions, she pressed on alone with her labour, only to be caught up in a dramatic snowfall sent as punishment. The weight of the deadly white cloak spelt her end, while the snow-covered pastures, alas, hardened into the glacier we see today.

She has not been alone in her icy tomb, as countless soldiers perished on the treacherous high-altitude terrain of the Marmolada during the First World War hostilities. The Austrians lost 300 alone in a single avalanche in December 1916. The demarcation line between Italy and the former Hapsburg Empire ran the length of the crest, and Austrian ingenuity led to the excavation in the glacier itself of the incredible City of Ice, a complex series of trenches and fortifications together with an astounding total of 12 km of tunnels deep in the eerie recesses. While the underground premises provided shelter from avalanches and enemy fire, survivors told of the uncanny pale blue light, then spine-chilling creaks and groans of the glacier in slow movement. The progressive retreat of the ice field of late has meant that poignant war remains continually come to light. Many of the victims of the conflicts and avalanches have been laid to rest in the Ossario (see Walk 29), the military mausoleum in the vicinity of Passo Pordoi.

In addition to the bus used at the walk end to return to the start point, the walk takes a cable-car to reach 2478m. Outside the operating period, you can follow path n.698 – though not a particularly inspiring way to climb almost 900m, mostly via ski slopes and service tracks, it shouldn't take more than 2hr 30min or so. A more attractive alternative is to start the walk from Passo Pordoi, then taking the steep 400m descent path to Lago di Fedaia, and from there the bus to Canazei.

STAGE ONE: TO PORTA VESCOVO (15MIN) THEN RIF. VIEL DEL PAN (1HR)

The cable-car from **Arabba** (1600m) takes its time climbing the approximately 900m, so there's plenty of time to admire the Dolomites north over Val Badia. Your arrival at the space-age station of **Porta Vescovo** ('the bishop's door', 2478m) on the tufaceous Padon ridge is greeted by the awe-inspiring sight of the Marmolada to the south. An earlier First World War cable-car ran this far to supply Austrian positions along the crest. Below the snack bar is a wooden sign for Viel del Pan and n.601. At a nearby junction you are pointed right for the clear if narrow path cutting southwest around the grassy mountainside; the magnificent Civetta soon comes into sight to

Access to start point:
The SS 48 and Passo Pordoi connect Val di Fassa and Arabba, which stands at the head of the Val Cordevole. Dolomiti Bus links Belluno with Arabba 12 months a year, with extensions to Corvara mid-June to mid-Sept, while the SAD services from Passo Pordoi and Corvara can be counted on from late June to mid-September. For the alternatives, Atesino buses connect Canazei and other towns in Val di Fassa with the Marmolada, namely Lago di Fedaia (mid-June to mid-Sept).
The cable-car used in Stage One from Arabba to Porta Vescovo runs from early July to the start of Sept.

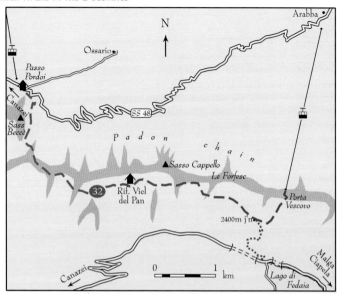

the southeast. The route is quite dramatic on this dizzy stretch over the dam, Lago di Fedaia, at the foot of the Marmolada, which cradles its glacier. Just over a quarter of an hour from Porta Vescovo, you join a broader path at a **2400m junction** (the left branch drops to Lago di Fedaia).

The Viel del Pan, n.601, coasts west for the most part and passes below a series of curious black lavic pinnacle formations, **Le Forfesc**, said to be the haunt of an ageing prince, Vögl delle Velme, when in a black mood. Legends and rumours were rife of an underground realm and fabulous treasure, peopled by subjects doomed never to see the light of day in return for never-ending riches.

Nearby two saddles in the crest afford marvellous views north to the Sella massif, topped by the pyramidal Boè peak. After skirting the base of castle-like Sasso Cappello (also spelt Sas Ciapel), you coast up to **Rif. Viel del Pan** (2431m). The family-run hut occupies a superb position directly opposite the Gran Vernel peak, while the crowds midsummer attest to the quality of the tasty local dishes served. (Note: the water is unsuitable for drinking here.)

STAGE TWO: TO PASSO PORDOI (45MIN)

West from **Rif. Viel del Pan** and set in the grassy flanks are more volcanic formations, reminiscent of Easter Island statues. Boulders of conglomerate flank the path, which is a little wider here as it doubles as access for the refuge's mini-tractor to bring up essential supplies. The Catinaccio group looms due west. About half an hour along, the path crosses the crest (northwest) to reach **Rif. Baita Fredarola** (2388m), opposite the monumental Sella massif. Now you need to head downhill via the wide track under a ski lift. However, don't miss a final brief detour up left to another wonderful lookout at a ski lift station, with vast views east to the Catinaccio, Sciliar and beyond, as well as Sassolungo-Sassopiatto at closer range. The main path rounds the base of Sass Beccè, home to a colony of romping marmots. The key road pass, **Passo Pordoi** (2239m), is just around the corner soon after a chapel, and you can return to **Arabba** by bus.

Tourist Office Arabba
tel. 0436-79130

Rif. Baita Fredarola
tel. 0462-602072
private, sleeps 36,
open 20/6–end Sept

Rif. Viel del Pan
tel. 0462-601720
private, sleeps 15,
open 20/6–20/9, also
May + Oct for meals

Casa Alpina (Passo Pordoi)
tel. 0462-601279
sleeps 45, open June to mid-Oct

Rif. Viel del Pan

33 – Civetta,
the Northwestern Flank

'The grand façade of the Civetta – a sheer, magnificent wall of upright precipice, seamed from crown to foot with thousands of vertical fissures, and rising in a mighty arch towards the centre – faces to the north-west, looking directly up the Cordevole towards Caprile, and filling in the the end of the valley as a great organ-front fills in the end of a Cathedral aisle.' (Amelia Edwards, 1872)

Walking time	7hr + 1hr for the Rif. Tissi detour
Walk distance	20km/12.4 miles
Difficulty	Grade 2
Ascent/descent	630m/1850m
Map	Tabacco n.025 or n.015 scale 1:25,000
Start point	Alleghe

On a calm night, it is said that church bells can be heard tolling eerily beneath the deep green waters of Alleghe's lake. They ring for the unburied victims of a disastrous landslide. At precisely two minutes past seven in the evening of January 11th, 1771, a huge rock slab from Monte Piz slid downwards barring Val Cordevole. It caused the river to flood and form a lake, the rockfall thus completely burying two hamlets and drowning two others in the process. The locals used to say that the old rooftops were distinctly visible beneath the surface when the waters were not ruffled or when the ice was perfectly transparent in winter. Strangely, the name of the present-day township of Alleghe comes from the Ladin 'a l'ega' ('on the water'), an ancient name referring to the confluence of several rivers and used long before the lake came into existence. A further curiosity of toponymy – the very river, the Cordevole, was so dubbed from 'cordubium' ('dubious heart') for the fear its violent currents and waves induced in those obliged to cross it.

These days Alleghe is a modest mountain resort that boasts an ice rink and cable-car. It lies in the imposing shadow of the phenomenal trident-shaped massif of the Civetta. The name actually means 'owl' in Italian, derived from local dialect. The 3220m of this Dolomite

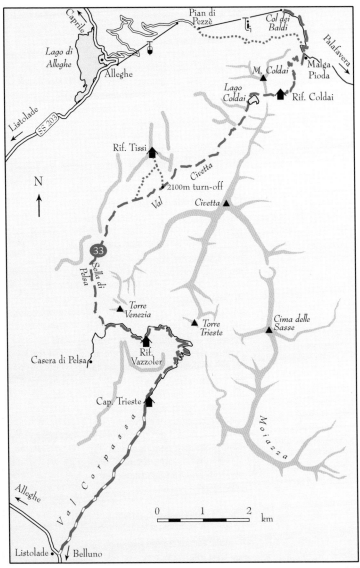

par excellence were first scaled in 1867 by the English climber Francis Fox Tuckett.

The Civetta's unequalled northwestern face is followed in its entirety on this tiring, though extremely rewarding, walk. Almost too long for a single day, it is also feasible in chunks from either direction. Awe-inspiring scenery is the theme of this walk, and variety comes in the form of lakes, far-off Dolomite groups, masses of flowered pasture slopes and shady woods alive with animal life, not to mention several hospitable manned huts encountered en route which make marvellous rest and refreshment stops.

Access to start point:
Alleghe is on the SS 203, and is well served by year-round Dolomiti Bus coaches from Belluno and Caprile.

The initial part of the walk makes use of two mechanised lifts: the Alleghe-Pian di Pezzè gondola cars and the connecting chair lift to Col dei Baldi generally operate from late June to mid-Sept. It is also possible to drive as far as Pian di Pezzè and take path n.564, which leads to Malga Pioda, close to Col dei Baldi. This means an additional 2hr but is helpful when the lifts are not operating.

STAGE ONE: VIA PIAN DI PEZZÈ AND COL DEI BALDI (15MIN) TO RIF. COLDAI (1HR 15MIN)

After the leisurely mechanised ascent from **Alleghe** (978m) via Pian di Pezzè (1470m) to **Col dei Baldi** (1922m) and its snack bar, turn right down the white gravel track. By all means cut the ensuing curve. The modest summer dairy farm **Malga Pioda** (1816m) is not far away (15min), along with the car park for traffic from Palafavera in Val Zoldana. Drinking water, refreshments and dairy produce (though not necessarily at bargain prices) can be got here. Now path n.556, broad at first, makes its way south-southwest via a wartime mule track in slow zigzags which take the sting out of the steep climb. At times it hugs the cliff face, a veritable rock garden. Just after the mechanised cableway that supplies the hut is the divine sun terrace of **Rif. Coldai** (2132m, also know as Rif. Sonino al Coldai), a fairly modern and comfortable hut wonderfully placed beneath M. Coldai and across the valley from the magnificent Pelmo. It also takes in the vast panorama with the 'minor' Dolomites such as the Bosconero group (east-southeast), Spiz di Mezzodì and San Sebastiano-Tamer (southeast/south-southeast).

STAGE TWO: VIA LAGO COLDAI (20MIN) TO THE RIF. TISSI 2100M TURN-OFF (1HR 10MIN)

From the hut, well-used path n.560 (or Alta Via 1) climbs due west to a wide neck, Forcella Coldai (2191m), overlooking the milky green lake and offering views of the Marmolada to the northwest. It's only a short drop to the shallow cirque housing **Lago Coldai** (2143m); its sandy shore and grassy hillock surrounds are great for picnics, a fact exploited by the intrusive flocks of yellow-beaked choughs that appear out of nowhere at the rustling of a plastic bag.

After looping round the tarn the path climbs south to the 2208m **Forcella Col Negro** (30min from Rif. Coldai). The marvellous elongated western face of the Civetta now comes into view in all its glory, the 'wall of walls'. In the distance, southwest, is the Pale di San Martino group, preceded in the foreground by Rif. Tissi on its isolated perch. The ensuing stretch is probably the most spectacular section of the itinerary. From the *forcella*, if there is minimal snow cover at the start of the season, by all means take the unnumbered path that cuts across the massive scree flows and occasional snow and ice patch above Val Civetta; otherwise stick to the official route that drops some 100m through a stony grass basin before ascending to the **Rif. Tissi 2100m turn-off** below Col Rean. In general the path is signed by old orange paint bands, along with the occasional blue triangle for the Alta Via 1. En route Alleghe and its lake come into view, as does the immense grey slab bordering it to the west, the remnant of the mountain that crashed down in the 18th century.

Torre Trieste on the Civetta

Side trip to Rif. Tissi (1hr return)

If the views to date have not proved satisfactory, follow the branch of n.560 that climbs 30min north to Cima di Col Rean. (Note that the timing for this recommended detour is not included in the total calculated for the walk.)

Rif. Tissi (2250m) is an excellent lookout for the Civetta western wall in its entirety, rising some 1200m from the scree base to a maximum of 3220m, virtually opposite the hut. The mountain's 'eye' or trademark pocket glacier, the Giazer, can be seen hanging onto the sheer rock. The vertical formations have been likened to a set of gigantic organ pipes. Moreover, the cross behind the building close to the near vertical cableway for transporting supplies affords a dizzying view of the plunge to Alleghe and vast views (southwest to north) of the San Martino group, Marmolada, Sella, Cunturines, Lagazuoi and Tofane, and even a glimpse of the Pelmo to the northeast.

To return to the main route, go the short way downhill to the signed junction where you are pointed right (sign for Rif. Vazzoler) to rejoin main path n.560 in Val Civetta, a short distance west of the **2100m turn-off**.

The Civetta viewed from the west

STAGE THREE: TO RIF. VAZZOLER (1HR 30MIN)

N.560 continues south-southwest dodging the enormous boulders that continue to detach themselves from the Civetta, and through undulating pasture basins run through with streams, resulting in varying degrees of marshiness. Sella di Pelsa (1954m) is followed by gradual descent to round the foot of magnificent Torre Venezia, renowned for its climbing routes. A rough farm track is joined for the final dusty 20min southeast to where **Rif. Vazzoler** nestles at 1714m in a wood of delicate larch trees. The impeccable old-style hut makes for a wonderful stop-over, its picnic tables looking onto the sheer ochre-tinted Torre Trieste, the imposing spread of the Moiazza group east-southeast, and Cima delle Sasse due east. A further attraction is the well-kept alpine flower rock garden, each species carefully labelled, and there is a chapel commemorating mountaineers who have lost their lives on the Civetta over the years.

STAGE FOUR: DESCENT TO CAPANNA TRIESTE (1HR) AND LISTOLADE (1HR)

Jeep track n.555 resumes eastwards, skirting the base of Torre Trieste, across several watercourses to zigzag easily downhill through spreads of dwarf mountain pines. You can see all the way down Val Corpassa to the cluster of houses at Listolade, backed by Monte Agner.

At **Capanna Trieste** (1135m), the track becomes a narrow surfaced road for a straightforward stroll to **Listolade** (701m) in Val Cordevole and the SS 203, from where you take the bus back to **Alleghe**.

Tourist Office Alleghe
tel. 0437-523333

Capanna Trieste
tel. 0437-660122
private, sleeps 20,
open May to early Oct

Rif. Coldai
tel. 0437-789160 CAI,
sleeps 89,
open 20/6–20/9

Rif. Tissi
tel. 0437-721644 CAI,
sleeps 54,
open 15/6–20/9

Rif. Vazzoler
tel. 0437-660008 CAI,
sleeps 80, open mid-
June to end Sept

34 – Pale di San Martino: A Circuit on the Altipiano

'The mountain-knot which raises its well-nigh perpendicular masses behind Primiero may be compared to a horseshoe from which protrude spikes of irregular length. The easiest paths, the only ones practicable for beasts of burden, wind round the base of the protuberances; the higher passes, fit for shepherds or foot-travellers, penetrate the recesses between the lofty spurs and cross the horseshoe itself. The former are not the least fascinating.

For this country owes its wonderful beauty in great part to the constantly recurring contrast between the tall bare cliffs of the great rock islands and the soft forms of the green hills which like a sea roll their verdurous forms between them.'
(D.W. Freshfield, 1875)

Walking time	5hr 30min
Walk distance	13km/8.1 miles
Difficulty	Grade 2–3
Ascent/descent	780m/780m
Map	Tabacco n.022 scale 1:25,000
Start point	Col Verde gondola lift departure

The multi-faceted Dolomite group known as the Pale di San Martino dominates both the market town of Fiera di Primiero and the trendy resort township of San Martino di Castrozza, which faces the sheer impressive western flanks. Referred to by Douglas Freshfield (1875) as a 'bevy of formidable giants', it encompasses a unique combination of soaring towers and points, some elegant rounded shapes, others severe pointed needles, hemming in a stone desert – a high-level plateau marked by gibbosity and karstic depressions, known locally as *buse* (literally 'holes'). These were the result of the movements of the thick ice sheet which covered the entire area until the end of the last ice age, some 10,000 years ago, and many harbour either unassuming lakes as well as the odd pocket glacier. The *altipiano* extends for around 20km² and rises to 2500–2800m above sea level.

This day walk consists of a marvellous circuit that takes in both the rolling rockscapes of the *altipiano*, which can seem very bare and uninviting in the summer, despite the crown of awe-inspiring peaks, along with a series of severely beautiful valleys, profound gashes that drop from the central platform, providing an excellent 'taste' of the group. A number of demanding climbs and descents are entailed, as well as a string of rock passages aided by cables. However, exposure is minimal, and

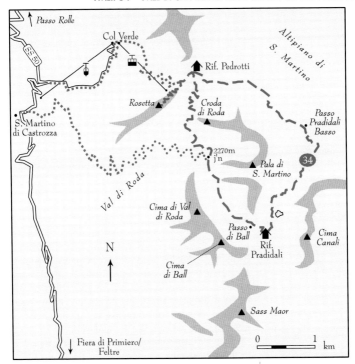

only youngsters or inexperienced walkers need a harness and karabiners.

The entire day is spent amongst rock environs luckily brightened by some stunning alpine flora – the rare bell-flower, *Campanula morettiana*, endemic to the Dolomites, gay yellow Rhaetian poppies and pink thrift, to name but a few. All are protected as they grow in the Parco Naturale Paneveggio–Pale di San Martino.

A warning is in order for the *altipiano*: treacherous fog and low cloud, fairly common occurrences, can transform a straightforward stroll into an exercise in orienteering as the undulating rocky surface has little in the way of recognisable features and it can be tricky getting your bearings. The main paths are marked by pyramidal stone cairns, red-white paint splashes and the occasional signpost, but the area should be avoided in unsettled weather. Moreover, walkers in early summer should expect to encounter remnant snow in the valleys. At the other extreme, remember to carry adequate drinking water and sun protection gear with high-factor sun cream.

Access to start point:
Atesina buses link San Martino di Castrozza with Trento and Feltre all year round in addition to an occasional link with Predazzo in Val di Fassa. By car take the SS 50. For the walk start, 5min on foot uphill from the town, the gondola lift to Col Verde and ensuing Rosetta cable-car are operational from 10 June to 10 October.

An alternative to the rather expensive mechanised ascents in Stage One can be found in Stage Two, but remember it adds a lot to both walking time and height gain and loss.

Stage One: via Col Verde to Rosetta arrival station (15min), ascent of Rosetta (40min return time) and to Rif. Pedrotti (10min)

The two-stage ascent from **San Martino di Castrozza** (1470m) via gondola car to **Col Verde** (1965m) then the sensational cable-car terminates at 2609m on the verge of the breath-taking plateau. Leave the main route straightaway and turn up right (southwest) on the clear, if unmarked, path towards the cross on the 2743m **Rosetta** peak (20min), a dizzy spot. Westwards over the township is the darker rock spread of the metamorphic Lagorai chain, and the Catinaccio peaks further back northwest, while far off are the ice-bound Ortles-Cevedale groups to the west-northwest and Brenta-Adamello to the west. On the other hand, in the San Martino group itself, the majestic Cimon della Pala rises northwest, and southeast is the Pala di San Martino then Cima di Ball, separated by the Passo di Ball.

Return to the main path and follow it to the spick and span **Rif. Pedrotti** (2578m). Recently subject to timely restructuring at the hands of the praiseworthy Trento branch of the Alpine Club, it was one of the earliest refuges in the Dolomites, originally constructed in 1889. Badly damaged during the First World War, it was rebuilt in 1921, enlarged in 1934, burnt down by German forces in 1943 and eventually brought back to life in 1952 – the usual story!

Stage Two: via Val di Roda 2270m junction (1hr), Passo di Ball (45min) and on to Rif. Pradidali (20min)

As per signposting, move off south on broad path, n.702, via Passo di Val Roda (2572m) for the drop down the dramatic flank to skirt the base of Croda di Roda. The bleached mountainsides contrast strongly with the dark, almost luscious green of the forested valleys far below, while the rock face closer at hand harbours a host of flowers such as saxifrages and thrift. This former mule track, which climbs from the outskirts of San Martino up the Val di Roda to the plateau, was the brain-child of a Dresden baron in 1905, when the area belonged to the Hapsburg Empire. As the story goes, the workers were paid by the metre rather than on a time basis, and ingeniously stretched out the path, judging from its interminable zigzags and all but imperceptible descent. Eventually, 300m lower, you reach Col delle Fede (2278m), a grassed outcrop once of importance for grazing, judging by its name. A level stretch leads around east now across a scree valley flanking the massive Pala di San Martino, offering a glimpse of a surviving pocket glacier. Not far on is the strategic **2270m junction** (1hr) for n.715, and where the following alternative route from San Martino joins up.•

Path n.715 breaks off south-southeast to climb steadily in the shade of a stunning array of spires and peaks: for the moment the most notable is Cima di Val di Roda (south-southwest). It narrows a little, cutting the mountainside at a constant height above the valley floor. Following a warning sign suggesting inexperienced walkers rope up and use karabiners is the start of a couple of stretches of guiding cable anchored to the rock, which should be tackled with the appropriate care. Difficulty is average in good conditions, and exposure minimal for experienced walkers. The going is very beautiful, and the path reappears for the final clamber to **Passo di Ball** (45min, 2443m), between Cima di Ball (southwest) and Cima Pradidali (northeast). Over to the east rises beautiful Cima Canali, while south is impressive Sass Maor and the Vette Feltrine. The pass was named in honour of John Ball, one of the initiators of Dolomite mountaineering.

N.715 continues in an easy descent eastwards dodging toppled boulders and scree to **Rif. Pradidali** (2278m, 20min), a very pleasant timber-panelled

•**Alternative ascent from San Martino to 2270m junction (2hr 15min)** One feasible alternative to the mechanised ascents is path n.702. It leaves San Martino (1470m) as a vehicle track in the vicinity of the gondola lift station, and heads southeast before becoming a path beneath the southern face of the Rosetta. Subsequently it climbs Val di Roda and joins the main route at the **2270m junction**, entailing a 800m climb and a total of 1hr extra.

The vast San Martino Altipiano, with the cable-car station and Rif. Rosetta

building that dates back to 1896, courtesy of the Dresden Alpine Club. Its name comes from the *prati gialli*, yellow meadows, south down the valley, so-called for the profusion of yellow poppies that unfailingly adorn the zone.

STAGE THREE: VIA PASSO PRADIDALI BASSO (1HR 20MIN) AND RETURN TO THE CABLE-CAR (1HR)

You leave the comfort of **Rif. Pradidali** to embark on an ascent of a desolate rubble valley that climbs back to the central plateau. Path n.709 is well waymarked and proceeds in stages past silted-up Lago Pradidali then a series of scree-strewn terraces, brightened by delightful concentrations of colourful blooms. There are good views onto the magnificent line-up of towers and spires to the west – outstanding are Cima Pradidali and Cima Immink. Around 2300m the route shifts northeast, with some trouble-free rock clambers. Turn-offs for Passo delle Lede and later Passo di Fradusta are ignored, and you keep left (northwest now) for the final climb to **Passo Pradidali Basso** (1hr 20min, 2704m) and a return to the strange landscape of the *altipiano*.

Close at hand is the glittering spread of the Fradusta glacier, sheltering out of the sun's grasp on the north-facing flank of the peak of the same name. It's worth detouring for 10min or so to the neighbouring col for a better look, along with a vast panorama taking in the distant Marmolada to the north.

For the return leg to the cable-car, take n.709 forking left (northwest). An initial briefly exposed stretch cuts across rock wall, then you make your way across the stone desert. Ahead northwest is Cimon della Pala, with Cima della Vezzana to its right, while Rif. Pedrotti is soon visible, with the Rosetta to its left. Keep a constant eye on waymarking and cairns as you negotiate the tiring ups and downs back to **Rif. Pedrotti** then the **cable-car** (1hr) once more.

If you happen to have missed the last car down, backtrack briefly for Passo di Rosetta and path n.701, an interesting and straightforward partially aided rock-based route that criss-crosses under the cable-car to Col Verde (1hr), from where you take the service track to **San Martino** (1hr).

Tourist Office S. Martino di Castrozza tel. 0439-768867

Rif. Pedrotti alla Rosetta tel. 0439-68308 CAI-SAT, sleeps 80, open 20/6–20/9

Rif. Pradidali tel. 0439-64180 CAI, sleeps 64, open 20/6–20/9

Fradusta glacier from Passo Pradidali Basso

35 – Pale di San Martino: Rif. Mulaz

The northern realms of the marvellous Pale di San Martino consist of elegant soaring pale towers, high-altitude passes and a web of crazy paths that zigzag up impossible scree slopes above lush pasture valleys. Nowadays a protected area under the auspices of the Parco Naturale Paneveggio–Pale di San Martino, it is home to chamois, marmots and legendary golden eagles.

Walking time	5hr 45min (less 45min if chair lift or bus used to Baita Segantini)
Walk distance	16.5km/10.2 miles
Difficulty	Grade 2
Ascent/descent	1200m/1200m (less 190m if chair lift or bus used to Baita Segantini)
Map	Tabacco n.022 scale 1:25,000
Start point	Passo Rolle

The destination of this walk, Rif. Mulaz, is superbly located at the head of a dramatic valley crowned with beautiful peaks. The establishment is more correctly known as Rif. Giuseppe Volpi al Mulaz, as it was named by the land-lords, the Venice branch of the Alpine Club, after the entrepreneur responsible for a great deal of the industrial development around the city in the 1920s, not to mention the world-famous film festival in 1932.

The itinerary is feasible for any walker fit enough to tackle steep terrain with a loose rock base and fair height gain and loss. Remember that the climb is tiring, especially under a blazing sun as there is no shade at all. On the other hand early summer walkers should expect snow cover on the upper reaches, especially in the proximity of Rif. Mulaz. Carry plenty of drinking water as well as sun protection. Chair lift, bus or private vehicle can be used in Stage One, shortening the walk by 45min.

A recommended follow-up to the walk is a visit to the park's visitors' centre and deer enclosure at Paneveggio, north of Passo Rolle. It is set on the edge of the famed Paneveggio forest. Dominated by towering thriving spruce, now fully recovered from the devastation of the war years, it once furnished special wood for string instruments, not to mention much-needed timber for the Venetian Republic.

STAGE ONE: PASSO ROLLE TO BAITA SEGANTINI (45MIN)

On the San Martino side of **Passo Rolle** (1980m), at the first bend with the chair lift, is the start of the dirt track n.710. The former Austrian military road climbs north at first before swinging east to pass close to Capanna Cervino (2082m). However, a more direct unmarked path leads straight up the grassy slopes following the chair lift. Marvellous views are glimpsed from the start, and in the meantime there are plenty of distractions in the way of alpenrose and thick masses of globe flowers that flourish in the marshy terrain. Photogenic restaurant **Baita Segantini** (2170m) and its lake come complete with a breathtaking array of light-grey peaks. Dominant is the slender point of Cimon della Pala, often referred to as the Matterhorn of the Dolomites and which shades the remnant Travignolo glacier; next is Cima della Vezzana and various peaks over the 3000m mark, culminating with M. Mulaz, to the northeast. Back the other way is the dark metamorphic Lagorai chain.

STAGE TWO: VIA PASSO DEL MULAZ (2HR 15MIN) TO RIF. MULAZ (15MIN)

From **Baita Segantini** the dirt track (closed to private traffic from here on) drops quickly into the head of Val Venegia, a pretty grazing valley clad with larches, whose lower reaches feature hospitable summer farms-cum-

Access to start point:
Passo Rolle can be reached by public transport (Atesina buses) from both San Martino di Castrozza as well as the opposite direction, Predazzo in Val di Fiemme, mid-June to mid-September. By car you'll need the SS 50 which runs from Feltre via San Martino then over to Predazzo. A dirt track leads from Passo Rolle to Baita Segantini, and it is open to private traffic.

A special Passo Rolle–Baita Segantini bus does daily runs from about 10/7 to 10/9, while the chair lift on the same tract usually covers the midsummer period, depending on the weather.

Spectacularly placed Rif. Mulaz

eateries. Path n.710 breaks off to the right, and some 30min down at 1950m you are directed right at a boulder (red arrow) for the start of the 600m climb, a stiff slog on loose stones. The ascent is relentless amidst glaring white rock; however, despite the stark scree ambience, wild flowers such as pink thrift and yellow Rhaetian poppies have taken root and stand out everywhere you look. At about 2400m the intermediate point for the refuge's mechanised cableway is passed and you enter a vast upper amphitheatre beneath Campanile di Val Grande and its orange-grey scree flows. The path struggles up the northern side over occasional grass patches where marmots have settled. A turn-off for Passo delle Farangole is ignored, then you're on the final leg to **Passo del Mulaz** (2hr 15min, 2619m).

This leads to the verge of a brand new valley and an inspiring view to the hut, with the sight of the majestic Civetta (east-northeast) a further plus beyond the Val di Biois.

It's an easy 15min drop to exemplary **Rif. Mulaz** (2571m). Constructed in 1907, it stands very close to what was then the Austrian confine and which now coin-

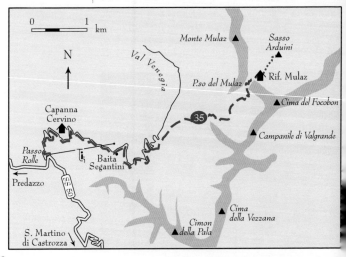

cides with the border between the Trento and Belluno provinces. The building faces the magnificent Cima del Focobon to the southeast (its name from 'good pasture'), whilst its neighbours are Cima di Campidol and Cima Zopel.•

STAGE THREE: RETURN TO BAITA SEGANTINI (2HR) THEN PASSO ROLLE (30MIN)

The way back via **Baita Segantini** to **Passo Rolle** is the same as the outward path.

•Extension to Sasso Arduini (20min return)
From **Rif. Mulaz** path n.753 detours briefly northeast to modest, rounded **Sasso Arduini** (2582m). It offers incredibly extensive and breathtaking views, especially of the Marmolada (north), Catinaccio (north-northwest) behind the long Costabella crest, and Tofane (northeast), to mention but a few. Sasso Arduini also harbours some exquisite king-of-the-Alps blooms.

Tourist Office S. Martino di Castrozza tel. 0439-768867

Capanna Cervino tel. 0439-769095 private, sleeps 18, open 20/6–20/9

Rif. Mulaz tel. 0437-599420 CAI, sleeps 70, open 20/6–20/9

At the head of Val Venegia, near Baita Segantini

36 – Latemar: Lago di Carezza and the Labyrinth

The Latemar is an imposing and severe massif that emerges from a thick forest of pines. Its airy culminating crest is a jagged line-up of slender eroded rock spires and towers, petrified dolls according to one imaginative tale.

Walking time	2hr 15min
Walk distance	8.5km/5.3 miles
Difficulty	Grade 1–2
Ascent/descent	450m/450m
Map	Tabacco n.029 scale 1:25,000
Start point	Grand Hotel Carezza

The name Latemar was probably given to the mountain by the 14th-century Ladin population – taken from 'mora' or 'mara' for the unusually abundant flows of scree it produces. In fact the massif is composed of limestone but run through by countless veins of metamorphic rock; the many contact lines and faults spell weak points, facilitating erosion. Its mineral content is high, and the northern sectors were mined at length, with settlements of German workers founded nearby. The Latemar was part of a massive volcano over 200 million years ago, preceding the formation of the Alps, its erstwhile centre at what is now the township of Predazzo in Val di Fiemme.

At the foot of the northern face a basin rimmed with pine trees harbours a delightful sparkling lake which reflects the mountain. Lago di Carezza/Karer See is renowned for its brilliantly coloured crystal-clear waters, qualities attributed by one legend to precious jewels buried in its sandy floor. However, another well-known Ladin tale tells of a graceful nymph who spent her days on the water's edge singing. She had the misfortune to attract a crafty wizard who schemed to carry her off; he forged a marvellous rainbow to distract her, on the advice of a famous witch from the Mugoni, on the Catinaccio group opposite. However, the plan went awry, the nymph was saved and, blind with anger, the wizard smashed the rainbow into smithereens. The pieces fell into the lake where the colours dissolved in the water and remained to dazzle visitors. In colder, more factual terms, the Lago di Carezza lies 1534m above sea level, is 250m long and 125m wide, while the depth varies between 5–7m, as it depends on the quantity of meltwater from snow that feeds it, in addition to underground sources. The best period to visit is early summer, when the lake is more likely to be full.

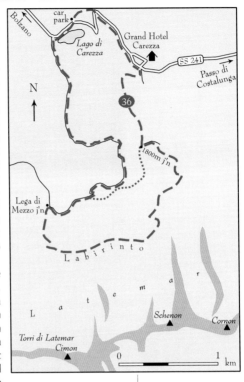

Thanks partly to the adjacent Catinaccio chain, a great attraction, this area was opened up to tourism in the mid-1850s when ingenious engineers cut a road through the dramatic red porphyry gorge Val d'Ega creating a link with Bolzano. Via the Passo di Costalunga it proceeds east to Val di Fassa. The Grand Hotel was inaugurated in 1896 and soon became the summer residence of glamorous Sissi (Empress Elizabeth) of the Austrian-Hungarian Empire. In the post World War One period, when the South Tyrol passed under Italian control, the establishment was popular with the foreign aristocracy and visitors such as Winston Churchill, who is remembered for his paintings. Another visitor was Agatha Christie, who set the conclusion to her 1927 thriller *The Big Four* on the renowned Labirinto (Labyrinth) route which runs below the Latemar's dramatic north face: 'We were hurried through the woods at a break-neck pace, going uphill the

Access to start point:
Grand Hotel Carezza/ Hotel Karer See, where the walk starts, is located 2.5km west of Passo di Costalunga/Karer Paß and can be reached from either Val di Fassa or Bolzano on the SS 241. SAD coaches serve the pass all year.

The Latemar seen from the Sciliar

whole time. At last we emerged in the open, on the mountain-side, and I saw just in front of us an extraordinary conglomeration of fantastic rocks and boulders. This must be the Felsenlabyrinth of which Harvey had spoken. Soon we were winding in and out of its recesses. The place was like a maze devised by some evil genie.'

A well-kept path these days, equipped with red arrows and cairns, it provides a leisurely half-day walk, and it is a good first walk in the Dolomites. **Warning:** rockfalls are not uncommon. Should the path be closed temporarily, you may have to be content with a lower variant – described at the end of Stage One.

Drinks and picnic supplies should be carried for the walk, though plenty of excellent eateries (such as Bei Toni) can be found in the vicinity of the Grand Hotel, not to mention guesthouses (such as Waldhaus).

STAGE ONE: FROM GRAND HOTEL CAREZZA VIA THE LABIRINTO (30MIN) TO LEGA DI MEZZO JUNCTION (45MIN)

Opposite the marvellous old-style **Grand Hotel Carezza** (1609m) is the start of a forestry track, marked n.18. A few metres along, a path (unmarked at first) breaks off right, crosses another track and proceeds to climb easily south through dense forest with plenty of red/white waymarking. The lilac flowers of adenostyles and their spreading leaves account for the undergrowth, as well as the occasional purple orchid. After some 30min uphill you arrive at a signed **1800m junction** – keep left. An opening in the wood shows the proximity of the towers and sheer flanks of the Latemar. Narrow path n.20 soon turns off right (southwest) to cross a silted basin at the foot of the mountain before commencing its gentle winding climb into the chaos of toppled boulders from ancient rockslides. The ground has been colonised by thick carpets of mountain avens, while streams of stones illustrate the interesting mix of light-coloured limestone interspersed with black fragments of volcanic origin.

The climb is gentle below the Latemar's crazily eroded spires, while back behind you the spread of the beautiful Catinaccio appears. The path passes directly below the main towers (Torri del Latemar) just before re-entering the wood and traversing several devastating rivers of scree through the trees. Close at hand are meadows and a huddle of timber huts on a forestry track, the **Lega di Mezzo junction** (Mitterleger, 1840m). Views back up to the vast multi-coloured scree flows from the Latemar's unstable flank are awe inspiring to say the least.•

STAGE TWO: DESCENT TO LAGO DI CAREZZA (45MIN) AND RETURN TO GRAND HOTEL CAREZZA (15MIN)

From the **Lega di Mezzo junction**, turn right via the wide forestry track for the leisurely stretch north in descent to the road. Here is **Lago di Carezza** (1519m) and its extraordinary colours, ensconced in the dark green fir forest. After a suitable exploration, cross over to the **car park** and kiosks for the start of path n.10 (signed for the Grand Hotel). It cuts up through wood before crossing the road and leading you on a pretty track back to the **Grand Hotel Carezza** (1609m).

•**Alternative route to Lega di Mezzo junction** If the Labirinto route is closed, from the **1800m junction** take the right branch. As n.21 it cuts west across the mountainside and in about 15min joins the forestry track a short way below the Lega di Mezzo junction.

Tourist Office Nova Levante/Welschnofen tel. 0471-613126

Grand Hotel Carezza/ Hotel Karer See tel. 0471-612090

Waldhaus (at the rear of Grand Hotel Carezza) tel. 0471-612121

37 – Catinaccio: the Inner Realms of the Rose Garden

Clearly visible from Bolzano railway station, this celebrated Dolomite group is primarily known in Italian as the Catinaccio, which derives from 'large basin or bowl', a reference to its innermost open shell-shaped formation. Its breathtaking rock spires and towers have naturally long attracted mountaineers. The first recorded ascent of the Catinaccio d'Antermoia dates back to 1878, to the credit of G. Santner, with the Torri del Vaiolet a matter of years later.

Walking time	5hr + 2hr for extension
Walk distance	13km/8.1 miles
Difficulty	Grade 2–3 (Grade 3 for the gully to Rif. Re Alberto I)
Ascent/descent	930m/930m + 360m for extension
Map	Tabacco n.029 or n.06 scale 1:25,000
Start point	Rif. Ciampediè

A long-gone legendary kingdom of dwarves ruled by kindly King Laurino once occupied an underground world of tunnels and caves filled with fabulous treasures deep in the rocky recesses of an enormous mountain. Outside wonderful gardens of red roses bloomed all year long, with nothing more than a delicate silk thread acting as the border. Laurino, alas, lost his heart to the beautiful Lombard Princess Similda, an outsider; and, when refused her hand in marriage, he kidnapped her by magic. Furious battles ensued, and in the end the princess was rescued and the dwarf king captured. After languishing for long years in prison, Laurino escaped and determined to cast a spell on his beloved roses, which had led the enemy to the entrance of his kingdom and betrayed him. Never again during day or night would they be seen in their glory, so he turned them to stone. But he forgot to mention dusk in his spell, and so every evening after sunset the red roses appear briefly in their glowing splendour for a matter of minutes prior to nightfall. This exquisite phenomenon is known evocatively in the local Ladin language as Enrosadira ('alpenglow'), whereas the mountain became known as the Rosengarten ('rose garden') by German visitors in late 19th century as the story spread.

The walk described here ventures into the dizzy rocky reaches of the group, touching on a number of huts which cater to the needs of the summer multitudes. Stage Three of the itinerary entails a steep gully climbed with the aid of a guiding cable. While not particularly exposed (climbing equipment is not necessary), it does mean a challenging hands-on clamber rated as Grade 3, and is unsuitable for inexperienced walkers. An alternative is the straightforward optional extension to Passo Principe and its hut, described after Stage Four.

It is advisable to embark on the walk as early as possible to avoid the inevitable midsummer crowds. A plethora of *rifugi* in the Catinaccio itself provide excellent accommodation. The usual gear is recommended for the blazing sun, which can make the route extremely hot because of the lack of shade, reflection off the bleached rock and lack of a breeze due to the towering rock walls all around. Under no circumstances should you embark on this ascent if a storm is brewing or underway as the

The inner realms of the Catinaccio

Access to start point:
The start point, Rif. Ciampediè, can be reached with the help of various mechanised means: the Vigo di Fassa to Ciampediè cable-car, which operates mid-June to mid-October, or a series of chair lifts from Pera di Fassa as far as Rif. Ciampediè. Moreover Rif. Gardeccia, a little further uphill, is served by an excellent mini-bus shuttle from Pera and Pozza di Fassa mid-June to mid-September.

To get to Val di Fassa by public transport you'll need either the Atesina buses from Trento or the SAD service from Bolzano via Passo di Costalunga/Karer Paß.

Likewise drivers will need the SS 48 via Val di Fiemme, branching off from the Trento-Bolzano valley at Ora/Auer, or the SS 241 from Bolzano via spectacular Val d'Ega/Eggen Tal and Passo di Costalunga.

metal fixtures attract lightning. Plenty of drinking water is needed. If cold, gloves can be a good idea to protect your hands from the cable in Stage Three.

The walk starts at a point accessible by cable-car, chair lift or mini-bus. To reach it on foot from Vigo di Fassa (1393m) take track and path n.544 near the cable-car station for the rather monotonous ascent via eroded terrain beneath the cables in 1hr 30min.

STAGE ONE: FROM RIF. CIAMPEDIÈ TO RIF. GARDECCIA (40MIN)

The cable-car from Vigo deposits you at the old-style refuge **Rif. Ciampediè** (1997m), which lies just inside the open southern edge of the Catinaccio, an amazing spot to start out from as the outlook embraces most of the group's main peaks. The name Ciampediè comes from the Ladin for 'field of God'.

Path n.540 heads west at first past Rif. Negritella before sauntering northwest through light woods of larch, alpenrose and juniper – home to shy roe deer. You also get a good look at the Dirupi di Larsec, due north, Cima Catinaccio and the soaring Torri del Vaiolet to the north-west. The first of the cluster of buildings soon encountered is Rif. Catinaccio, not long before **Rif. Gardeccia** (1950m) and the shuttle bus terminal. A cluster of modest shops can be found nearby, with souvenirs, groceries and even fresh bread.

STAGE TWO: ASCENT TO RIF. VAIOLET (45MIN)

Popular route north n.546 (a jeep-width track) passes Rif. Stella Alpina and the last of the trees before climbing into the rock dominated landscape, where myriad wild flowers stand out against the bleached stones. The tall rock barrier across the valley is tackled in wide curves that take the sting out the otherwise steep climb, however it does not mitigate the strength of the sun's rays on a still morning. You emerge on a platform at Rif. Preuss, essentially an eatery, next door to the rambling and recently renovated historic **Rif. Vaiolet** (2243m). This curious name is derived from the ancient Ladin for 'cleft' or 'split', to describe the rocky towers.

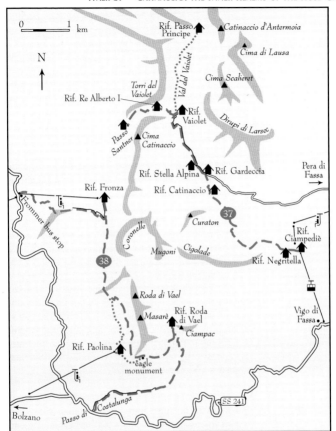

STAGE THREE: VIA RIF. RE ALBERTO I (1HR) TO PASSO SANTNER (20MIN)

From **Rif. Vaiolet** take n.542 due west up the broad rocky gully beneath the cable for the upper refuges' mechanised cableway. Clearly marked with red painted arrows and stripes, the path zigzags up the steep rock flank to the first of several long tracts of well-anchored cable to be tackled with due care. A trickling stream keeps you company, as do some startlingly colourful rock flowers

Tourist Office Vigo
di Fassa
tel. 0462-764093

Rif. Catinaccio
tel. 0368-7600700
private, sleeps 30, open
end May to end Sept

Rif. Ciampediè
tel. 0462-764432 CAI-
SAT, sleeps 26,
open 7/6–10/10

Rif. Gardeccia
tel. 0462-763152
private, sleeps 44,
open June to 10/10

Rif. Negritella
tel. 0462-764097
private, sleeps 15,
open 20/6–20/9

Rif. Passo Principe
tel. 0462-764244
private, sleeps 14,
open 25/6–30/9

Rif. Passo Santner
tel. 0471-642230
private, sleeps 8,
open 23/6–30/9

Rif. Re Alberto
tel. 0462-763428
private, sleeps 65,
open 25/6–25/9

such as yellow Rhaetian poppies, sky blue king-of-the-Alps and delicate pink alpine rock jasmine.

After a good 1hr climbing and 400m of ascent is **Rif. Re Alberto I** (2621m) and its diminutive snow-melt lake in a lunar setting surrounded by a crown of majestic rock towers. Strategically situated for the rock climbers who throng these mountains, it is placed directly at the foot of three of the magnificent dizzy spires of the Torri del Vaiolet, which stand out distinctly: (left to right) Torre Delago, named after the Innsbruck climber first to reach the 2780m top in 1895; Torre Stabele, for the Tyrolean guide who scaled its 2805m in 1892; and Torre Winkler, in memory of the intrepid high-school student who climbed solo to the 2800m point in 1887 at the age of 18. The atmosphere of this silent amphitheatre, the Gartl, is both unworldy and magical. The hut was named in honour of the Belgian King Albert I, a keen mountaineer who scaled numerous peaks in the company of the local expert and guide Tita Piaz in the early 1900s, and is still run by Piaz descendents.

A short detour (north) is scenic Passo di Laurino. While proceeding uphill the path curves around south-west heading for **Passo Santner** (2741m) at the foot of Cima Catinaccio, to its south, and the Croda di Re Laurino to the north. The low-set building of Rif. Passo Santner, unique in all respects, does not come into view until the very last minute. The outdoor loo, for a start, rates an indisputable 10 for its all-round panorama. The position is spectacular on the plunging western edge of the Catinaccio, high above the meadows that slope down to Passo di Costalunga and the Latemar to the south, the Sciliar (northwest), as well as the township of Bolzano (west-northwest) and the snow-capped Ortles-Cevedale chains beyond.

STAGE FOUR: DESCENT TO RIF. VAIOLET (1HR)
Backtrack as per the ascent route.

Extension: ascent to Passo Principe (2hr return time)
From **Rif. Vaiolet** (2243m) well-trodden path n.584 leads northwards following the broad principal, innermost

valley of the Catinaccio, Val del Vaiolet. Walkers who make an early start have a good chance of meeting the staff ferrying supplies by trail bike and backpack to **Passo Principe** (2599m, 1hr) and the hut of the same name, perched precariously under the crumbling rock face of Cima Valbona. However, your attention is immediately taken by the solid mass of the neighbouring Catinaccio d'Antermoia which rises to a height of 3002m to the east. To the north, on the other hand, is the huge scree-filled amphitheatre that precedes the Molignon. Return to **Rif. Vaiolet** the same way.

STAGE FIVE: RETURN VIA RIF. GARDECCIA (35MIN) TO RIF. CIAMPEDIÈ (40MIN)

As per the ascent.

Rif. Ciampediè on the edge of the Catinaccio

Rif. Stella Alpina
tel. 0462-763270
private, sleeps 28,
open June–Oct

Rif. Vaiolet
tel. 0462-763292 CAI-SAT, sleeps 140,
open 20/6–30/9

38 – Catinaccio: Sentiero del Masaré

Amongst the most popular destinations for summer walkers and climbers is the beautiful Catinaccio group, known to German speakers as the Rosengarten in memory of a legendary dwarf king whose renowned garden of red roses flourished miraculously on the barren mountain flanks (see Walk 37).

Walking time	4hr (less if chair lifts are used)
Walk distance	11.5km/7.1 miles
Difficulty	Grade 1–2
Ascent/descent	750m/750m
Map	Tabacco n.029 scale 1:25,000
Start point	Passo di Costalunga

A saunter along the Sentiero del Masaré, otherwise known as the Hirzelweg, beneath the imposing western rim of the soaring Catinaccio group, is an easy affair, with vast horizons visible and plenty of other Dolomite groups to admire. The 5km route is so-named in memory of the Leipzig publisher who ideated it in 1904, and follows the natural lay of the mountain in the shape of an elongated horizontal layer-cum-ledge, making for simple walking.

The walk described here (see map for walk 37) consists of a straightforward ascent on a good path before the level scenic tract, terminating with a steepish

Picnickers at Rif. Roda di Vael

drop to road level again. Families with young children may prefer to avoid ascent and descent altogether and limit themselves to easy terrain. This is possible thanks to the chair lift for Rif. Paolina, a couple of kilometres west of Passo di Costalunga, then another chair lift from Rif. Fronza down to Frommer. Thus the walk entails little over 1hr on foot.

STAGE ONE: FROM PASSO DI COSTALUNGA, ASCENT TO RIF. RODA DI VAEL (1HR 30MIN)

From **Passo di Costalunga** (1745m), alongside the Pensione Rosengarten, track n.548/552 strikes out north initially, its tarmac surface quickly giving out to dirt. At a 1830m fork (15min), n.548 branches off right to climb past a drinking fountain and summer huts before reverting to a path at 2000m. Light mixed wood is traversed as well as crumbly mountain flanks, the unstable beds that underlie the main upper dolomite rock. The far-off Marmolada comes into view to the east. You veer north for the zigzag climb through thinning flowered pasture toward rockscape to join the upper path (n.549). A right turn will take you to white-washed **Rif. Roda di Vael** (2280m) in its scenic saddle, with marvellous views to the Sella (northeast) and the Marmolada (east). Vaster views are obtainable from the 2316m hump known as Ciampac, at the rear of nearby snack bar Baita Pederiva. At a closer range to the north are the Mugoni, once a favourite haunt of witches who threw wild parties, during which the height of entertainment involved hurling flaming wheels onto the Cigolade crest, whose name means not surprisingly, burnt. Peace-loving marmots have since moved in.

STAGE TWO: TRAVERSE VIA EAGLE MONUMENT (20MIN) TO RIF. FRONZA (1HR10MIN)

Backtrack briefly to where you joined n.549 and stroll on south-southwest. This stretch is justifiably immensely popular; a broad path, it coasts between 2200 and 2300m, so you have ample opportunities to admire the changing views. The Pale di San Martino are visible southeast, while the sweep of the Latemar massif to the

Access to start point:
By public transport Passo di Costalunga/Karer Paß can be reached from Bolzano/Bozen 12 months a year via spectacular Val d'Ega/ Eggen Tal courtesy of the SAD buses, which also connect with Val di Fassa. For the final link in the walk, a twice-daily service covers the Frommer–Passo di Costalunga section from late June to mid-September.

Drivers will need the SS 241 from Bolzano, or the same road if approaching via Vigo di Fassa in the east.

The Paolina chair lift operates 1/6–15/10, and the chair lift from Rif. Fronza to Frommer runs from early June to the end of October.

south is reflected in the brilliant multi-coloured waters of the lake at its foot.

Where the path rounds the southernmost point of the Masaré, a bronze **eagle monument** stands on a grassy knoll in honour of Theodor Christomannos, a Viennese entrepreneur whose brainchild was the 1909 construction of the Great Dolomite Road linking Bolzano and Cortina, not to mention the stately Grand Hotel Carezza below.

(The nearby fork off left, n.539, leads to **Rif. Paolina** and its chair lift, 2125m.)

Stick to the upper path, mostly north now towards the massive red bulk and sheer 400m face of the Roda di Vael. The path will eventually drop briefly to be joined by the variant from Rif. Paolina. Keep right for the final stretch beneath the Coronelle to popular **Rif. Fronza** (2339m) in its marvellously panoramic setting. It is also referred to by its original name, Kölner Hütte, as it was erected by the Cologne Alpine Club back in 1889. The old-style rambling building can be better appreciated towards evening, when things quieten down.

Stage Three: descent to Frommer (1hr)

For those who do not opt for the chair lift descent, back along the broad main path is the turn-off for n.2c, the steep 600m drop to Frommer. After following a jeep-width track, a shorter path branches off on its own for the decisive descent from a rock to meadowy environs.

Frommer (1743m) is a good place for a meal or refreshments, as well as catching the bus back to **Passo di Costalunga**. (A further lift continues down to the Rosengarten guesthouse not far from Welschnofen/Nova Levante.)

Note: in the absence of a bus, allow just over 1hr for the 6km road.

Tourist Office Nova Levante/Welschnofen tel. 0471-613126

Tourist Office Vigo di Fassa tel. 0462-764093

Rif. A. Fronza alle Coronelle/Kölner Hütte tel. 0471-612033 CAI, sleeps 63, open 23/6–25/9

Rif. Paolina tel. 0471-612008 private, sleeps 15, open June–end Oct

Rif. Roda di Vael tel. 0462-764450 CAI-SAT, sleeps 50, open 20/6–30/9

39 – Brenta Group: Rif. Tuckett and ai Brentei Tour

Walking time	5hr 30min
Walk distance	18km/11.2 miles
Difficulty	Grade 2
Ascent/descent	492m/1407m
Map	Alpenvereinskarte n.51 Brentagruppe 1:25,000 or Tabacco n.10 scale 1: 50,000
Start point	Grostè gondola lift station, Campo Carlo Magno

Geographically the Brenta Dolomites are quite distinct from the rest, located west of the Trento-Bolzano valley and adjacent to the glacier-bound metamorphic Adamello range. However their geological composition and consequently appealing physical morphology with needle-thin formations and soaring towers is undeniably Dolomitic. This beautiful chain extends for a length of 40km and a width of 12km, and is blessed with myriad spectacular peaks around the 3000m mark. International mountaineering tourism was launched here in 1864 when John Ball crossed the Bocca di Brenta and wrote it up in the British press. Francis Fox Tuckett made history soon afterwards by carrying out the first traverse of the group. Together with Freshfield and Devouassoud he also held the record for scaling Cima Brenta (3150m), then thought to be the highest peak in the range. Nowadays the area comes under the Parco Naturale Adamello-Brenta.

Trendy town and world famous ski resort Madonna di Campiglio is to be found at the base of the Brenta's western flanks, and offers straightforward access to the paths and climbing routes thanks to well-placed lifts. Huts are not lacking either, so you can always drop in for a high-altitude lunch or refreshment during walks.

'Through breaks in the forest the glacier-crowned crags of the Cima di Brenta were now seen for the first time, followed on the north by an array of slender obelisks, beaks, and crooked horns, the strangeness of which would, but for a long experience in dolomite vagaries, have made us doubt our eyes.' (Douglas Freshfield, 1875)

The route that follows is spectacular, straightforward and highly recommended, though preferably not in peak season as the area is understandably very popular. A lift is used for Stage One, though an alternative route on foot is also given.

Stage One: gondola lift to Passo del Grostè (10min)

The **Grostè gondola lift** (1646m) departs in the vicinity of **Campo Carlo Magno**, named for the legendary passage of Charlemagne. The lift provides a leisurely trip east-southeast towards the stony landscapes of the northern realms of the Brenta Group. Nondescript **Passo del Grostè** (2442m), equipped with a restaurant, is the key passage to the vast undulating eastern sector of the group, and was thus described by Freshfield: 'The rocks fall away from the top towards the Flavona Alp in a series of advancing courses of massive masonry, like the sides of a Greek theatre.'

Alternative on foot to Passo del Grostè (2hr 15min)

Forestry track marked n.315 from the **Grostè gondola station** ascends steadily eastwards traversing wood then open rock in the shade of the Pietra Grande massif, characterised by sloping rock strata. You transit via **Rif. Graffer** (2261m) before a final steep climb to the actual **Passo del Grostè** (2490m).

Stage Two: traverse to Rif. Tuckett & Sella (1hr 30min)

Path n.316 strikes out southwest away from the pass and its ski-scarred surrounds into more varied landscapes, approaching the more spectacular central part of the Brenta. It is a magnificent route, level at first. Ahead (south-southwest) is majestic Cima Tosa, the highest of the Brenta Dolomites at 3159m, its upper face adorned with hanging glaciers. About 20min over stony wastes, a turn-off for Rif. Graffer is passed, then you embark on a series of ups and downs over karstic terrain and long-fallen boulders beneath all manner of spires, towers and needles which make up the western flanks of the group

Access to start point:
Atesina buses provide daily Trento–Madonna di Campiglio links all year long. The resort can also be reached from the Val di Sole in the north – by bus from Malè railway station courtesy of the Ferrovia Trento-Malè (FTM).

Car owners need the SS 45bis then the SS 237 west from Trento to Tione, followed by the SS 239 north along the Val Rendena to Madonna di Campiglio. Otherwise take the road from Dimaro in Val di Sole.

The two-section Grostè gondola lift, which starts out 2km north of Madonna di Campiglio, operates 24/6–17/9. At the conclusion of the itinerary, the taxi service from Rif. Vallesinella to Madonna di Campiglio can be used midsummer, and means cutting 1hr off the walk time.

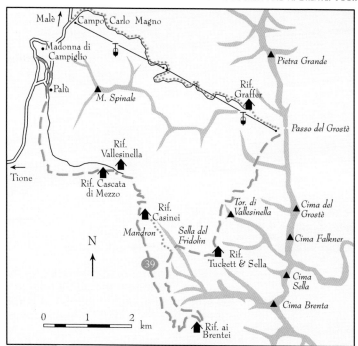

The most notable are the Torrione di Vallesinella and the Castelletto Inferiore on the final stretch south to superbly situated **Rif. Tuckett & Sella** (2272m). Here you can enjoy freshly baked carrot cake while drinking in the simply glorious location at the mouth of a valley overlooked by crazy finger points and headed by the Bocca del Tuckett and its conical glacier. The buildings are dominated by Punta Massari to the south, while westwards over Val Rendena is the extensive spread of the ice-bound Presanella–Adamello range.

The twin huts have been beautifully renovated in simple alpine style by the Trentino section of the Alpine Club. The slightly older building, inaugurated in 1906 in honour of Quintino Sella, who founded the Italian Alpine Club, was succeeded only a year later by the Berliner

Rif. Tuckett & Sella

Hütte, courtesy of the German Club. This was later renamed for pioneer British mountaineer Tuckett.

(A quick exit to Rif. Casinei is feasible from here by way of path n.317 – allow 1hr.)

STAGE THREE: VIA SELLA DEL FRIDOLIN (30MIN) TO RIF. AI BRENTEI (1HR)

Path n.328 climbs west at first, threading its way through a labyrinth of gigantic boulders that dwarf walkers. You are afforded bird's-eye views onto a vast river of pebbles and gravel borne by glacier meltwater. The water obstructed by the rockslide goes underground to emerge downhill in the vicinity of the waterfalls.

Gradual descent through low cover of dwarf mountain pine precedes grassy flower-studded **Sella del Fridolin** (2143m). Soon the path bears south over slippery sloping rock slabs run through with channelling where rainwater has dissolved the limestone. 40min from Rif. Tuckett you join n.318 from Rif. Casinei (a direct exit is possible here) and enter Val Brenta for a mostly level stretch.

Half an hour on, a steep cliffside is traversed with the aid of cables. This is followed by a shallow gorge complete with madonna shrine, then a short rock tunnel. A panoramic climb leads into the narrowing valley, beneath the western walls of Punta di Campiglio. The refuge building and chapel soon come into sight under the massive soaring bulk of Crozzon di Brenta (right) and Cima Tosa (left), their summits clutching at pockets of snow and ice, remnant hanging glaciers. A red arrow indicates a brief detour down right for 'acqua' – fresh spring water – it is worth filling your bottle as the nearby hut's supply is undrinkable due to its glacial origin.

Rif. Alberto e Maria ai Brentei (2187m), renowned old-style establishment, was run until recently by Bruno Detassis, a foremost mountaineer who opened up over 100 climbing routes between the 1930s and 1960s. His son, a qualified guide, is now in charge.

STAGE FOUR: DESCENT TO RIF. CASINEI (50MIN) AND RIF. VALLESINELLA (30MIN)

Sentiero Violi (path n.391) plunges west down a rubble slope to join a lower variant from Val Brenta Alta. It makes its way north at the foot of cliffs and crosses the Mandron, a pastoral clearing, before reaching **Rif. Casinei** (1826m).

From here you head valleywards on the zigzags of n.317 in shady wood and through grazing land, and should reach **Rif. Vallesinella** (1513m) and its huge car park in half an hour.

STAGE FIVE: WATERFALLS AND RETURN TO MADONNA DI CAMPIGLIO (1HR)

At **Rif. Vallesinella** you can collapse into a taxi for the 5km back to town, but it's a pity to miss the waterfalls. So take the unsurfaced road through lovely wood, and turn down left for signed **Rif. Cascata di Mezzo** (1400m), set close to crashing waterfalls. Cascata di Sotto, a lower fall, is a short stroll away. From the refuge a dirt track heads off west at first, curving north to Palù, where you join an asphalted road for the rest of the way through the outskirts of **Madonna di Campiglio** (1522m).

Tourist Office Madonna di Campiglio
tel. 0465-442000

Rif. Maria e Alberto ai Brentei
tel. 0465-441244 CAI , sleeps 100,
open 20/6–20/9

Rif. Casinei
tel. 0465-442708
private, sleeps 60,
open 10/6–10/10

Rif. Graffer tel. 0465-441358 CAI-SAT, sleeps 70,
open 20/6–20/9

Rif. Tuckett & Sella
tel. 0465-441226, CAI-SAT, sleeps 130,
open 1/6–30/9

Rif. Vallesinella
tel. 0465-442883
private, sleeps 30,
open 20/6–20/9

40 – Brenta Group: the Glories of Val d'Ambiez

The fascinating Val d'Ambiez runs for 12km through the southern part of the beautiful Brenta Dolomite group. A first impression is of a deep river-cut cleft between steep cliffs, however the upper part has retained more ancient features and presents an ample amphitheatre, or cirque, whose rounded shape is due to moulding by long-gone glaciers. This is surmounted by an awesome crown of typically spectacular Dolomite peaks.

Walking time	6hr 30min (reduced to 2hr 20min if jeep taxi used)
Walk distance	17km/10.5 miles
Difficulty	Grade 1-2
Ascent/descent	1560m/1560m (reduced to 600m if jeep taxi used)
Map	Alpenvereinskarte n.51 Brentagruppe 1:25,000 or Tabacco n.10 scale 1: 50,000
Start point	Baesa

Val d'Ambiez attracts far fewer visitors than the more accessible central Brenta section (see Walk 39), and reserves plentiful delights in the shape of an intriguing fossil area and excellent range of wild flowers and animals – birds of prey, herds of chamois, mouflon and deer. Hunting is still carried out here, authorised and strictly controlled by the Parco Naturale Adamello-Brenta. Pastoral activities have long been practised here, as suggested by the valley's name – Ambiez is believed to come from the Celtic for either 'good pasture' or 'canal carrying water to a mill'.

No particular difficulty is entailed in the walk, except for the hefty 1600m height gain and loss, though this is reducible to 600m if you weaken and take a jeep taxi as far as Rif. Al Cacciatore. The closest village is San Lorenzo, well equipped with shops for picnic supplies, whereas Baesa, the start point, has only a bar-restaurant. Two hospitable huts are encountered during the walk, though neither has drinkable tap water, so take your own. Binoculars are another must.

STAGE ONE: ASCENT TO RIF. AL CACCIATORE (2HR 30MIN)

Baesa (850m) consists of a car park and Bar Ristoro Dolomiti, located at the foot of cliffs and the narrow opening that announces the start of Val d'Ambiez. During the 16th–17th centuries a *lazaretto* for isolating people afflicted with the plague or cholera evidently stood here. You need to follow n.325 (the rough road), closed to unauthorised traffic, which climbs for 9km. About 1km uphill at **Pont de le Scale** (915m) either take the path that follows the right-hand bank of Torrente d'Ambiez or stick to the road which crosses to the left side. There's little

Access to start point:
Baesa is 3km from the village of San Lorenzo in Banale, found in turn on the SS 421, which branches north from the SS 45bis near the Terme di Comano spa resort and proceeds to Molveno.

Occasional Atesina buses via Ponte Arche (from Trento and Madonna di Campiglio) run to S. Lorenzo, from where authorised jeep taxis depart at set times (July to 1st week Sept) for Baesa and Rif. Al Cacciatore. Owners of private vehicles can park at either S. Lorenzo or Baesa.

Fossilised Megalodonts, Val d'Ambiez

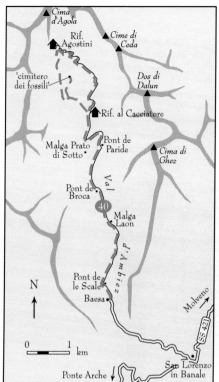

difference time-wise. The valley is quite closed in here, with no hint at all of the glories ahead! Via the path some half hour on after a clearing you cross the watercourse and pass **Malga Laon** (1110m, 50min) to rejoin the road, equipped with concrete runners now. The wood is essentially beech here. Pretty cascades precede **Pont de Broca** (1304m) and the start of a canyon where the road has been hewn out of the rock face. Soon afterwards the valley finally starts to widen and you glimpse Dolomite towers ahead. At a further bridge, **Pont de Paride** (1547m, 1hr 45min), the two magnificent Cima di Ceda peaks come into view to the north. The road shortly commences a series of steep ramps bearing left up to pasture clearings which sport ruined huts and a link to a modern summer farm, Malga Prato di Sotto. A final effort brings you out on the verge of the vast high-level amphitheatre surrounded by sheer rock walls and a semi-circle of soaring peaks. The dwarfed shape of Rif. Agostini is just visible northwest on a rocky spur. Close at hand is **Rif. Al Cacciatore** (1820m), a comfortable family-run establishment named for hunters (*cacciatore*). The nearby chapel set among low dwarf mountain pine is dedicated to Sant'Ubaldo, the protector of hunters. Your chances are good of spotting mouflon and chamois on the surrounding lightly wooded rock flanks.

STAGE TWO: VIA 'CIMITERO DEI FOSSILI' TO RIF. AGOSTINI (1HR 30MIN)

Leave the hut and take path n.325 (Sentiero Dallago), which branches left (northwest) off the jeep track amidst bushy low heather, alpenrose and dwarf mountain pines. A little over 5min along, as the path starts veering left (south), leave it momentarily for a 20min detour. A faint unmarked trail climbs northwest towards a terrace. Past a spring and over horizontal rock strata towards the base of a second terrace, you come into the so-called '**cimitero dei fossili**' ('cemetery of fossils'). A very interesting karstic zone with parallel ripple-edged decorations where surface water has sliced through the limestone, the pale slabs here are embedded with dense concentrations of

Rif. Agostini at the head of Val d'Ambiez

massive fossilised bivalves, Megalodont shells. They resemble hoofprints of some gigantic goat or deer, and are believed to date back 220 million years. Moreover, the rock crannies where precious rock debris and soil have collected have been colonised by mountain avens and even velvety edelweiss. Return to the main path the same way.

Path n.325 resumes its northern direction and heads across more fissured karstic terrain with an ever-improving panorama of the cirque and its old moraine ridges now colonised by vegetation. The path joins the jeep access track for the last leg to the marvellous position at the foot of the eastern wall of Cima d'Ambiez occupied by **Rif. Agostini** (2410m). It would appear to have been constructed purposefully adjacent to two impressive fallen rock forms which double as a practice wall for climbers in training. However they made their sudden appearance amidst an almighty crash of cascading stones at dawn on July 18th 1957, much to the astonishment of the occupants of the building, as the blocks came miraculously to a halt just metres from them. The chapel on a belvedere behind the hut provides long-reaching views south to Lake Garda and M. Baldo. There's no lack of picnic spots in the vicinity, and you'll be kept company by inquisitive alpine choughs.

STAGE THREE: RETURN VIA RIF. AL CACCIATORE (50MIN) TO BAESA (1HR 40MIN)

Take the jeep track for the subsequent 4km descent. It meanders pleasantly via ample grazing basins and passes a summer farm a short way before **Rif. Al Cacciatore** (1820m).

The rest of the way down to **Baesa** you need to follow the same route as Stage One, the ascent.

Tourist Office S. Lorenzo in Banale tel. 0465-734040

Rif. Agostini tel. 0465-734138 CAI-SAT, sleeps 56, open 20/6–20/9

Rif. Al Cacciatore tel. 0465-734141 private, sleeps 46, open 20/6–20/9 + weekends May and Oct

ITALIAN–GERMAN–ENGLISH GLOSSARY

acqua potabile	Trinkwasser	drinkable water
acqua non potabile	Kein Trinkwasser	non-drinkable water
agriturismo	Jausenstation	farm selling meals and products
aiuto!	zu Hilfe!	help!
altipiano, altopiano	Hochebene	high-level plateau
aperto/chiuso	geöffnet/geschlossen	open/closed
autostrada	Autobahn	motorway subject to toll
bivacco	Biwak	unmanned hut for mountaineers
cabinovia, telecabina	Kabinenbahn	gondola car lift
cadin/ciadin		cirque or valley, sometimes peak
campanile		rock tower, spire
capitello		shrine
cascata	Wasserfall	waterfall
casera		hut or dairy farm
caserma		barracks
castello	Schloss	castle
cengia	Band	ledge
cima	Gipfel	mountain peak
croce	Kreuz	cross
destra/sinistra	rechts/links	right/left
diga	Staumauer	dam
fermata	Haltestelle	bus stop
fiume	Fluß	river
forcella	Scharte	mountain pass for walkers
funivia	Seilbahn	cable-car
galleria	Tunnel	tunnel
ghiacciaio	Gletscher	glacier
giro	Rundgang	circuit
locanda	Gasthof	guesthouse

malga	Alm	high altitude summer farm
nevaio	Firnfeld	firn/snow field
ometto	Steinmann	cairn
orario	Fahrplan	timetable or opening hours
ospizio	Hospiz	hospice
pericolo	Gefahr	danger
piz	Spitze	peak
ponte	Brücke	bridge
previsioni del tempo	Wettervorhersage	weather forecast
rifugio	Hütte	manned mountain hut with food/accommodation
rio	Bach	stream
scorciatoia	Abkürzung	short cut
seggiovia	Sessellift	chair lift
sella	Sattel	saddle
sentiero	Weg, Steig	path
sopra		lower/below
sorgente	Quelle	spring
sotto		upper/above
stazione ferroviaria	Bahnhof	railway station
teleferica		mechanised goods cableway
torre	Turm	tower
torrente	Wildbach	mountain stream
trattoria		modest restaurant
val, valle	Tal	valley
vedretta		hanging glacier
vetta	Gipfel	peak
via ferrata	Klettersteig	aided climbing route

FURTHER READING

Bosellini, Alfonso (1989)
La storia geologica delle Dolomiti, Edizioni Dolomiti, Pordenone

Bruun, Bertel et al (1992)
Birds of Britain and Europe, Hamlyn, London

Edwards, Amelia (1986)
Untrodden Peaks and Unfrequented Valleys, Virago Press, London, reprint of
Longman's 1873 edition

Freshfield, Douglas W. (1875)
Italian Alps, Longman, Green, and Co., London

Gilbert, Josiah and Churchill, G.C. (1864)
*The Dolomite Mountains. Excursions through Tyrol, Carinthia, Carniola, and
Friuli*, Longman, Green, Longman, Roberts, & Green, London

Grey-Wilson, Christopher and Blamey, Marjorie (1995)
Alpine Flowers of Britain and Europe, HarperCollins Publishers, London

Schaumann, Walter (1984)
La Grande Guerra 1915/18, Ghedini & Tassotti Editori, Bassano del Grappa, 5
vols (Italian translation of *Schauplätze des Gebirgskrieges*)

NOTES

NOTES

LISTING OF CICERONE GUIDES

NORTHERN ENGLAND
LONG DISTANCE TRAILS
- THE DALES WAY
- THE ISLE OF MAN COASTAL PATH
- THE PENNINE WAY
- THE ALTERNATIVE COAST TO COAST
- NORTHERN COAST-TO-COAST WALK
- THE RELATIVE HILLS OF BRITAIN
- MOUNTAINS ENGLAND & WALES
  VOL 1 WALES
  VOL 2 ENGLAND

CYCLING
- BORDER COUNTRY BIKE ROUTES
- THE CHESHIRE CYCLE WAY
- THE CUMBRIA CYCLE WAY
- THE DANUBE CYCLE WAY
- LANDS END TO JOHN O'GROATS
  CYCLE GUIDE
- ON THE RUFFSTUFF -
  84 BIKE RIDES IN NORTH ENGLAND
- RURAL RIDES NO.1 WEST SURREY
- RURAL RIDES NO.1 EAST SURREY
- SOUTH LAKELAND CYCLE RIDES
- THE WAY OF ST JAMES
  LE PUY TO SANTIAGO - CYCLIST'S

LAKE DISTRICT AND MORECAMBE BAY
- CONISTON COPPER MINES
- CUMBRIA WAY & ALLERDALE
  RAMBLE
- THE CHRONICLES OF MILNTHORPE
- THE EDEN WAY
- FROM FELL AND FIELD
- KENDAL - A SOCIAL HISTORY
- A LAKE DISTRICT ANGLER'S GUIDE
- LAKELAND TOWNS
- LAKELAND VILLAGES
- LAKELAND PANORAMAS
- THE LOST RESORT?
- SCRAMBLES IN THE LAKE DISTRICT
- MORE SCRAMBLES IN THE
  LAKE DISTRICT
- SHORT WALKS IN LAKELAND
  BOOK 1: SOUTH
  BOOK 2: NORTH
  BOOK 3: WEST
- ROCKY RAMBLER'S WILD WALKS
- RAIN OR SHINE
- ROADS AND TRACKS OF THE
  LAKE DISTRICT
- THE TARNS OF LAKELAND
  VOL 1: WEST
- THE TARNS OF LAKELAND VOL 2:
  EAST
- WALKING ROUND THE LAKES
- WALKS SILVERDALE/ARNSIDE
- WINTER CLIMBS IN LAKE DISTRICT

NORTH-WEST ENGLAND
- WALKING IN CHESHIRE
- FAMILY WALKS IN FOREST OF
  BOWLAND

- WALKING IN THE FOREST OF
  BOWLAND
- LANCASTER CANAL WALKS
- WALKER'S GUIDE TO LANCASTER
  CANAL
- CANAL WALKS VOL 1: NORTH
- WALKS FROM THE LEEDS-
  LIVERPOOL CANAL
- THE RIBBLE WAY
- WALKS IN RIBBLE COUNTRY
- WALKING IN LANCASHIRE
- WALKS ON THE WEST PENNINE
  MOORS
- WALKS IN LANCASHIRE WITCH
  COUNTRY
- HADRIAN'S WALL
  VOL 1 : THE WALL WALK
  VOL 2 : WALL COUNTRY WALKS

NORTH-EAST ENGLAND
- NORTH YORKS MOORS
- THE REIVER'S WAY
- THE TEESDALE WAY
- WALKING IN COUNTY DURHAM
- WALKING IN THE NORTH PENNINES
- WALKING IN NORTHUMBERLAND
- WALKING IN THE WOLDS
- WALKS IN THE NORTH YORK
  MOORS BOOKS 1 AND 2
- WALKS IN THE YORKSHIRE DALES
  BOOKS 1,2, AND 3
- WALKS IN DALES COUNTRY
- WATERFALL WALKS - TEESDALE &
  HIGH PENNINES
- THE YORKSHIRE DALES
- YORKSHIRE DALES ANGLER'S GUIDE

THE PEAK DISTRICT
- STAR FAMILY WALKS PEAK
  DISTRICT/STH YORKS
- HIGH PEAK WALKS
- WEEKEND WALKS IN THE PEAK
  DISTRICT
- WHITE PEAK WALKS
  VOL.1 NORTHERN DALES
  VOL.2 SOUTHERN DALES
- WHITE PEAK WAY
- WALKING IN PEAKLAND
- WALKING IN SHERWOOD FOREST
- WALKING IN STAFFORDSHIRE
- THE VIKING WAY

WALES AND WELSH BORDERS
- ANGLESEY COAST WALKS
- ASCENT OF SNOWDON
- THE BRECON BEACONS
- CLWYD ROCK
- HEREFORD & THE WYE VALLEY
- HILLWALKING IN SNOWDONIA
- HILLWALKING IN WALES VOL.1
- HILLWALKING IN WALES VOL.2
- LLEYN PENINSULA COASTAL PATH
- WALKING OFFA'S DYKE PATH
- THE PEMBROKESHIRE COASTAL
  PATH

- THE RIDGES OF SNOWDONIA
- SARN HELEN
- SCRAMBLES IN SNOWDONIA
- SEVERN WALKS
- THE SHROPSHIRE HILLS
- THE SHROPSHIRE WAY
- SPIRIT PATHS OF WALES
- WALKING DOWN THE WYE
- A WELSH COAST TO COAST WALK
- WELSH WINTER CLIMBS

THE MIDLANDS
- CANAL WALKS VOL 2: MIDLANDS
- THE COTSWOLD WAY
- COTSWOLD WALKS
  BOOK 1: NORTH
  BOOK 2: CENTRAL
  BOOK 3: SOUTH
- THE GRAND UNION CANAL WALK
- HEART OF ENGLAND WALKS
- WALKING IN OXFORDSHIRE
- WALKING IN WARWICKSHIRE
- WALKING IN WORCESTERSHIRE
- WEST MIDLANDS ROCK

SOUTH AND SOUTH-WEST ENGLAND
- WALKING IN BEDFORDSHIRE
- WALKING IN BUCKINGHAMSHIRE
- CHANNEL ISLAND WALKS
- CORNISH ROCK
- WALKING IN CORNWALL
- WALKING IN THE CHILTERNS
- WALKING ON DARTMOOR
- WALKING IN DEVON
- WALKING IN DORSET
- CANAL WALKS VOL 3: SOUTH
- EXMOOR & THE QUANTOCKS
- THE GREATER RIDGEWAY
- WALKING IN HAMPSHIRE
- THE ISLE OF WIGHT
- THE KENNET & AVON WALK
- THE LEA VALLEY WALK
- LONDON THEME WALKS
- THE NORTH DOWNS WAY
- THE SOUTH DOWNS WAY
- THE ISLES OF SCILLY
- THE SOUTHERN COAST TO COAST
- SOUTH WEST WAY
  VOL.1 MINEH'D TO PENZ.
  VOL.2 PENZ. TO POOLE
- WALKING IN SOMERSET
- WALKING IN SUSSEX
- THE THAMES PATH
- TWO MOORS WAY
- WALKS IN KENT BOOK 1
- WALKS IN KENT BOOK 2
- THE WEALDWAY & VANGUARD WAY

SCOTLAND
- WALKING IN THE ISLE OF ARRAN
- THE BORDER COUNTRY -
  A WALKERS GUIDE
- BORDER COUNTRY CYCLE ROUTES

- BORDER PUBS & INNS -
  A WALKERS' GUIDE
- CAIRNGORMS, WINTER CLIMBS
  5TH EDITION
- CENTRAL HIGHLANDS
  6 LONG DISTANCE WALKS
- WALKING THE GALLOWAY HILLS
- WALKING IN THE HEBRIDES
- NORTH TO THE CAPE
- THE ISLAND OF RHUM
- THE ISLE OF SKYE A WALKER'S
  GUIDE
- WALKS IN THE LAMMERMUIRS
- WALKING IN THE LOWTHER HILLS
- THE SCOTTISH GLENS SERIES
  1 - CAIRNGORM GLENS
  2 - ATHOLL GLENS
  3 - GLENS OF RANNOCH
  4 - GLENS OF TROSSACH
  5 - GLENS OF ARGYLL
  6 - THE GREAT GLEN
  7 - THE ANGUS GLENS
  8 - KNOYDART TO MORVERN
  9 - THE GLENS OF ROSS-SHIRE
- SCOTTISH RAILWAY WALKS
- SCRAMBLES IN LOCHABER
- SCRAMBLES IN SKYE
- SKI TOURING IN SCOTLAND
- THE SPEYSIDE WAY
- TORRIDON - A WALKER'S GUIDE
- WALKS FROM THE WEST HIGHLAND
  RAILWAY
- THE WEST HIGHLAND WAY
- WINTER CLIMBS NEVIS & GLENCOE

IRELAND
- IRISH COASTAL WALKS
- THE IRISH COAST TO COAST
- THE MOUNTAINS OF IRELAND

WALKING AND TREKKING IN
THE ALPS
- WALKING IN THE ALPS
- 100 HUT WALKS IN THE ALPS
- CHAMONIX TO ZERMATT
- GRAND TOUR OF MONTE ROSA
  VOL. 1 AND VOL. 2
- TOUR OF MONT BLANC

FRANCE, BELGIUM AND
LUXEMBOURG
- WALKING IN THE ARDENNES
- ROCK CLIMBS BELGIUM & LUX.
- THE BRITTANY COASTAL PATH
- CHAMONIX - MONT BLANC
  WALKING GUIDE
- WALKING IN THE CEVENNES
- CORSICAN HIGH LEVEL ROUTE:
  GR20
- THE ECRINS NATIONAL PARK
- WALKING THE FRENCH ALPS: GR5
- WALKING THE FRENCH GORGES
- FRENCH ROCK
- WALKING IN THE HAUTE SAVOIE
- WALKING IN THE LANGUEDOC
- TOUR OF THE OISANS: GR54
- WALKING IN PROVENCE
- THE PYRENEAN TRAIL: GR10
- THE TOUR OF THE QUEYRAS
- ROBERT LOUIS STEVENSON TRAIL

- WALKING IN TARENTAISE &
  BEAUFORTAIN ALPS
- ROCK CLIMBS IN THE VERDON
- TOUR OF THE VANOISE
- WALKS IN VOLCANO COUNTRY

FRANCE/SPAIN
- ROCK CLIMBS IN THE PYRENEES
- WALKS & CLIMBS IN THE PYRENEES
- THE WAY OF ST JAMES
  LE PUY TO SANTIAGO - WALKER'S
- THE WAY OF ST JAMES
  LE PUY TO SANTIAGO - CYCLIST'S

SPAIN AND PORTUGAL
- WALKING IN THE ALGARVE
- ANDALUSIAN ROCK CLIMBS
- BIRDWATCHING IN MALLORCA
- COSTA BLANCA ROCK
- COSTA BLANCA WALKS VOL 1
- COSTA BLANCA WALKS VOL 2
- WALKING IN MALLORCA
- ROCK CLIMBS IN MAJORCA, IBIZA &
  TENERIFE
- WALKING IN MADEIRA
- THE MOUNTAINS OF CENTRAL
  SPAIN
- THE SPANISH PYRENEES GR11
  2ND EDITION
- WALKING IN THE SIERRA NEVADA
- WALKS & CLIMBS IN THE PICOS DE
  EUROPA
- VIA DE LA PLATA

SWITZERLAND
- ALPINE PASS ROUTE, SWITZERLAND
- THE BERNESE ALPS A WALKING
  GUIDE
- CENTRAL SWITZERLAND
- THE JURA: HIGH ROUTE & SKI
  TRAVERSES
- WALKING IN TICINO, SWITZERLAND
- THE VALAIS, SWITZERLAND -
  A WALKING GUIDE

GERMANY, AUSTRIA AND
EASTERN EUROPE
- MOUNTAIN WALKING IN AUSTRIA
- WALKING IN THE BAVARIAN ALPS
- WALKING IN THE BLACK FOREST
- THE DANUBE CYCLE WAY
- GERMANY'S ROMANTIC ROAD
- WALKING IN THE HARZ
  MOUNTAINS
- KING LUDWIG WAY
- KLETTERSTEIG NORTHERN
  LIMESTONE ALPS
- WALKING THE RIVER RHINE TRAIL
- THE MOUNTAINS OF ROMANIA
- WALKING IN THE SALZKAMMERGUT
- HUT-TO-HUT IN THE STUBAI ALPS
- THE HIGH TATRAS

SCANDANAVIA
- WALKING IN NORWAY
- ST OLAV'S WAY

ITALY AND SLOVENIA
- ALTA VIA - HIGH LEVEL WALKS
  DOLOMITES
- CENTRAL APENNINES OF ITALY

- WALKING CENTRAL ITALIAN ALPS
- WALKING IN THE DOLOMITES
- SHORTER WALKS IN THE
  DOLOMITES
- WALKING ITALY'S GRAN PARADISO
- LONG DISTANCE WALKS IN ITALY'S
  GRAN PARADISO
- ITALIAN ROCK
- WALKS IN THE JULIAN ALPS
- WALKING IN SICILY
- WALKING IN TUSCANY
- VIA FERRATA SCRAMBLES IN THE
  DOLOMITES

OTHER MEDITERRANEAN
COUNTRIES
- THE ATLAS MOUNTAINS
- WALKING IN CYPRUS
- CRETE - THE WHITE MOUNTAINS
- THE MOUNTAINS OF GREECE
- JORDAN - WALKS, TREKS, CAVES ETC.
- THE MOUNTAINS OF TURKEY
- TREKS & CLIMBS WADI RUM
  JORDAN
- CLIMBS & TREKS IN THE ALA DAG
- WALKING IN PALESTINE

HIMALAYA
- ADVENTURE TREKS IN NEPAL
- ANNAPURNA - A TREKKER'S GUIDE
- EVEREST - A TREKKERS' GUIDE
- GARHWAL & KUMAON -
  A TREKKER'S GUIDE
- KANGCHENJUNGA -
  A TREKKER'S GUIDE
- LANGTANG, GOSAINKUND &
  HELAMBU TREKKERS GUIDE
- MANASLU - A TREKKER'S GUIDE

OTHER COUNTRIES
- MOUNTAIN WALKING IN AFRICA -
  KENYA
- OZ ROCK – AUSTRALIAN CRAGS
- WALKING IN BRITISH COLUMBIA
- TREKKING IN THE CAUCASUS
- GRAND CANYON & AMERICAN
  SOUTH WEST
- ROCK CLIMBS IN HONG KONG
- ADVENTURE TREKS WEST NORTH
  AMERICA
- CLASSIC TRAMPS IN NEW ZEALAND

TECHNIQUES AND
EDUCATION
- SNOW & ICE TECHNIQUES
- ROPE TECHNIQUES
- THE BOOK OF THE BIVVY
- THE HILLWALKER'S MANUAL
- THE TREKKER'S HANDBOOK
- THE ADVENTURE ALTERNATIVE
- BEYOND ADVENTURE
- FAR HORIZONS - ADVENTURE
  TRAVEL FOR ALL
- MOUNTAIN WEATHER

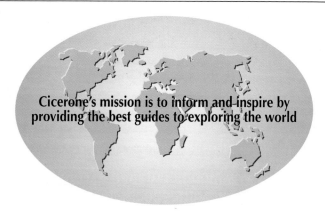

Cicerone's mission is to inform and inspire by providing the best guides to exploring the world

Since its foundation over 30 years ago, Cicerone has specialised in publishing guidebooks and has built a reputation for quality and reliability. It now publishes nearly 300 guides to the major destinations for outdoor enthusiasts, including Europe, UK and the rest of the world.

Written by leading and committed specialists, Cicerone guides are recognised as the most authoritative. They are full of information, maps and illustrations so that the user can plan and complete a successful and safe trip or expedition – be it a long face climb, a walk over Lakeland fells, an alpine traverse, a Himalayan trek or a ramble in the countryside.

With a thorough introduction to assist planning, clear diagrams, maps and colour photographs to illustrate the terrain and route, and accurate and detailed text, Cicerone guides are designed for ease of use and access to the information.

If the facts on the ground change, or there is any aspect of a guide that you think we can improve, we are always delighted to hear from you.

Cicerone Press
2 Police Square Milnthorpe Cumbria LA7 7PY
Tel:01539 562 069   Fax:01539 563 417
e-mail:info@cicerone.co.uk   web:www.cicerone.co.uk

CICERONE